A STUDY OF THE
BOOK OF NUMBERS

With Us in the Wilderness

LAUREN CHANDLER

LifeWay Press®
Nashville, Tennessee

Published by LifeWay Press® • © 2021 Lauren Chandler

ISBN: 978-1-0877-0078-6
Item: 005823707
Dewey decimal classification: 222.14
Subject heading: BIBLE. O.T. NUMBERS—HISTORY OF BIBLICAL EVENTS / GOD / EXODUS, THE

To order additional copies of this resource, write LifeWay Church Resources Customer Service; One LifeWay Plaza; Nashville, TN 37234-0113; FAX order to 615.251.5933; call toll-free 800.458.2772; email orderentry@lifeway.com; or order online at LifeWay.com.

Printed in the United States of America

LifeWay Women Publishing,
LifeWay Church Resources,
One LifeWay Plaza,
Nashville, TN 37234-0152

EDITORIAL TEAM,
LIFEWAY WOMEN
PUBLISHING

Becky Loyd
Director, LifeWay
Women

Tina Boesch
Manager, LifeWay
Women Bible Studies

Sarah Doss
Team Leader, LifeWay
Women Bible Studies

Erin Davis
Elizabeth Hyndman
Content Editors

Erin Franklin
Production Editor

Chelsea Waack
Graphic Designer

Lauren Ervin
Cover Designer

TABLE OF CONTENTS

ABOUT THE AUTHOR

Lauren Chandler is a wife and mother of three. Her husband, Matt Chandler, serves as the lead teaching pastor at The Village Church in Dallas, Texas. Lauren is passionate about writing, music, and leading worship, not only at The Village Church, but also for groups across the country. The Lord has taken Matt and Lauren on a challenging journey, beginning with the November 2009 discovery of a malignant brain tumor in Matt. The Lord has been infinitely merciful to provide peace and comfort in uncertainty and joy in times of victory and healing. Lauren and her family have been given a deeper trust in clinging to the Lord and His cross during this appointed season of valleys and storms.

Session One

INTRODUCTION

The LORD spoke to Moses
in the wilderness of Sinai . . .

NUMBERS 1:1a

Welcome to the *With Us in the Wilderness* Bible study! Each week, I've provided some discussion questions here to get the conversation started. Feel free to discuss what you learned throughout the week of study, ask any questions you may have, and share what God is teaching you.

DISCUSSION QUESTIONS

What drew you to this study? What do you hope to learn?

What comes to mind when you consider the Book of Numbers?

In the Book of Numbers, we see that God didn't remove His tabernacle from the center of the camp even though the people were rebellious. What might that tell us about God's character and how He feels about His people?

In our introductory teaching time, we talked about three themes we'll unpack in our study—comfort, warning, and hope. Of the three, which description most resonated with you? Why?

Teaching sessions available for purchase or rent at *LifeWay.com/WithUsInTheWilderness*

Session Two

HOLY GOD, HOLY PEOPLE

The LORD bless you and keep you;
the LORD make his face to shine upon you
and be gracious to you;
the LORD lift up his countenance upon you
and give you peace.
"So shall they put my name upon the
people of Israel, and I will bless them."

NUMBERS 6:24-27

DAY ONE
WHERE WE FIND OURSELVES

Pause. Breathe. Pray.

Sister, you are so welcome to this space in whichever state you find yourself: hungry to grow in your knowledge of the Lord through Scripture, limping in your own wilderness, or somewhere in-between. My prayer is that you make time, not to have all the right answers and all the blanks filled in, but to encounter the Living God in the study of His Word. He knows just what you need. I am praying He provides that for you here.

Where do you find yourself? Hungry? Limping? A little of both?

What would you like the Lord to do for you in the next seven sessions?

Write a simple prayer to the Lord asking Him to make His presence known to you as you study.

Every time I visit a new city or town, I look at a map to familiarize myself with the area. Which way is north? In what part of the city am I? How far away am I from _____? Understanding my geographical context helps me navigate the unfamiliar. Thus, I think it's a good use of our time together to take a moment to orient ourselves in the context of Numbers so we can navigate what might be an unfamiliar part of Scripture.

List the first five books of the Bible.

1.

2.

3.

4.

5.

These books are called the Pentateuch (also known as the Torah). Look up _Pentateuch_ in a dictionary and write what you find here:

Pretty self-explanatory, right? The Pentateuch is more than just the beginning of the Bible; it provides the framework for what we read in the rest of the Old Testament and beyond. In the New Testament, we see how Jesus came to fulfill all that was promised in and pointed to in these first five books.

Let's do a little review of each book (or a brief introduction for those who are new to the Pentateuch).[1]

GENESIS: A STORY OF BEGINNINGS

Genesis is a book of beginnings—the beginning of creation and of mankind. It tells the story of creation, mankind's fall into sin and death and God's plan of redemption through Abraham and his descendants.[2]

Turn to Genesis 12:1-3 (ESV) and fill in the blanks below.

*Now the L*ORD *said to Abram, "Go from your country and your kindred and your father's house to the land that I will show you. And I will make of you a great _____, and I will _____ you and make _____ _____ great, so that you will be a _____. I will _____ those who _____ you, and him who _____ you I will _____, and in you all the _____ of the_____ shall be _____."*

Abram's call (God later changed his name to Abraham) will be important to remember in our study of Numbers. We will see this promise come true in various ways among Abraham's descendants, the Israelites.

Abraham's family tree is quite complicated. The branches get a little confusing, especially since two of his granddaughters-in-law had a reproductive showdown. We will do our best to trace this family's somewhat sordid story and hopefully find comfort that our own family's history isn't the only story with scandalous plotlines. As we do, we will see that God can use it all for His glory.

Turn to the Scripture reference under each box on the next page and write the person's name that belongs there. (Hint: once you get to Jacob's sons, it will be easiest to follow the numbers!)

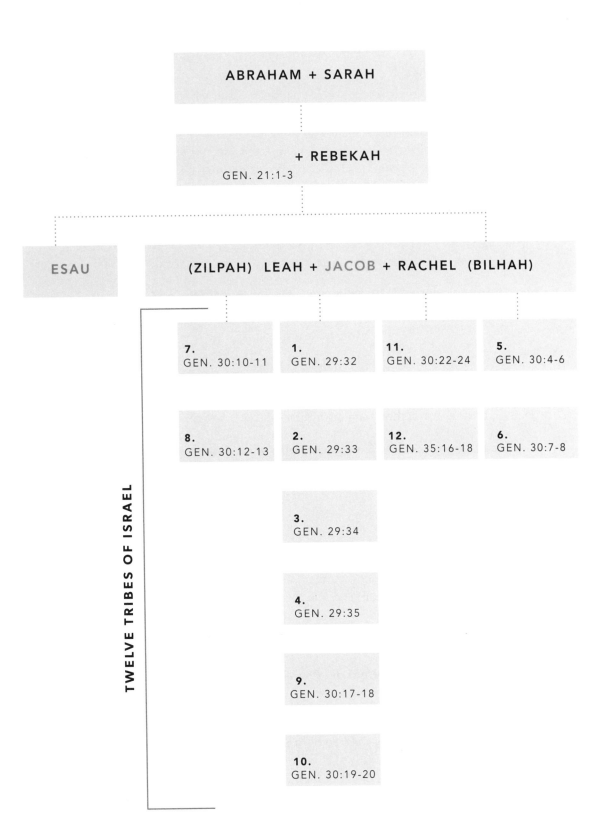

ABRAHAM + SARAH

+ REBEKAH
GEN. 21:1-3

ESAU

(ZILPAH) LEAH + JACOB + RACHEL (BILHAH)

7.
GEN. 30:10-11

1.
GEN. 29:32

11.
GEN. 30:22-24

5.
GEN. 30:4-6

8.
GEN. 30:12-13

2.
GEN. 29:33

12.
GEN. 35:16-18

6.
GEN. 30:7-8

3.
GEN. 29:34

4.
GEN. 29:35

9.
GEN. 30:17-18

10.
GEN. 30:19-20

TWELVE TRIBES OF ISRAEL

I hope you were able to keep straight all the wives, wives' servants, and whose children belonged to whom! You might be wondering a few things. First, what about Esau's children? Although Esau was the firstborn, he gave up that right for a bowl of stew (Gen. 25:29-34). Yep, this was not an even (nor wise) exchange. Esau was notorious for following his physical compulsions no matter the cost. Jacob, on the other hand, was notorious for being sneaky. In fact, he stole his brother's blessing by deceiving his father so the birthright and blessing followed Jacob's line, not Esau's. Are you starting to feel better about your own family drama? Second, why were they called the twelve tribes of Israel instead of the twelve tribes of Jacob? I'll let you dig for the answer.

Turn to Genesis 35:10. What accounts for this difference?

Genesis closes with the children of Israel (a.k.a. Jacob) living in the land of Egypt. Through another complicated series of events, Joseph (number eleven) was put in a position of honor and power in Egypt and saved his father, brothers, and their families from ruin.

Read Genesis 50:24-25 and summarize what Joseph asked his family to do for him.

EXODUS: A STORY OF DELIVERANCE

Exodus opens with the descendants of Jacob (a.k.a. Israel) living in Egypt and being fruitful and multiplying (i.e. having lots of children). The freedom they enjoyed didn't last long. A king arose who forgot about Egypt's friendly alliance with Joseph. Instead, he perceived Joseph's family as foes.

Read Exodus 1:8-14. What did Pharaoh do to the people of Israel?

Moses was one of the many children born to the people of Israel. He will be an important character in our study of Numbers. Moses' first forty years of life are worth a whole Bible study alone, but for the sake of time, I will summarize his story: Moses was an unlikely candidate whom God chose to lead His people out of slavery in Egypt, through the wilderness, and into the promised land.

The Book of Exodus is named after the Israelites' departure (or exodus) from Egypt and the tyranny of Pharaoh. Exodus closes with the people of Israel out of Egypt and in the wilderness of Sinai. They received the Ten Commandments (Ex. 20), built the tabernacle (Ex. 25–31) (more on this later), and were poised to follow God's lead through a cloud by day and fire by night (Ex. 13:21).

LEVITICUS: GUIDE TO LIVING IN THE LAND

I'm sure you are probably intimately acquainted with the Book of Leviticus. I imagine it's your favorite part of a Bible reading plan! I hope you can hear the sarcasm because I am laying it on thick! While Leviticus isn't necessarily the most enjoyable book to read in the Bible, it does provide a picture of how serious God is about holiness and how He desires His people to live holy lives.

Among other things, Leviticus is a book of Law. Take a moment and consider our own laws and regulations. What is the purpose of law?

As God's people transitioned from slaves in a foreign land to free people in a foreign desert, why would they need laws to be spelled out so specifically?

In the Book of Leviticus, the Lord gave instructions to Moses about how God's people were to live, including: sacrifices, offerings, worship, the priesthood, ceremonial cleanness, the Day of Atonement, holy feasts, holy days, and the Year of Jubilee. This isn't a book of random rules or hoops God created for His people to jump through. Through the law, God set the standard of living for the flourishing of humanity. What makes this even more amazing is He knew His children would not be able to keep the law on their own, so He provided a way of atonement through sacrifices and offerings. His goal is to dwell among His people. In order for a holy God to live with sinful humans, we must be made holy. Leviticus showed Israel how.

NUMBERS: WILDERNESS WANDERINGS

Spoiler alert! Here's a brief overview of our study, but don't be too disappointed. We will unearth much more gold in this book.

Numbers opens in the wilderness of Sinai with God telling Moses to take a military census of the people. They were readying themselves to enter the promised land. However, as a consequence of their lack of faith, they wandered in the wilderness for forty years. The generation that had been delivered from Egypt died in the wilderness (Num. 32:13). Praise the Lord the story doesn't end there! God still had a plan for His children. He ordered another military census of the new generation. Numbers closes with Israel positioned to settle in the promised land.

> **As the Israelites stood on the edge of the promised land, which part of God's call of Abraham (Gen. 12:2-3) might have come to mind?**

DEUTERONOMY: MOSES' FINAL WORDS

The fifth and final book of the Pentateuch, Deuteronomy, is Moses' last charge to Israel. It is a series of sermons and prophetic poems written to the children of Israel as they were about to inhabit the land God promised to Abraham.

Like a good grandfather, Moses reminded the Israelites of God's faithfulness, despite the previous generation's rebellion and lack of faith. He urged them to remember, love, trust, and obey the Lord so that it might go well for them in this new land. The end of the book marks the end of one era and the beginning of another.

> **What event is recorded in Deuteronomy 34?**

> **Describe the impact of this event on the people of Israel.**

Moses died before the people went into the promised land. God chose Joshua to lead the people in Moses' place.

At the end of our study of Numbers, you might be a little perturbed that Moses didn't make it. Moses learned a lot of leadership lessons the hard way. And the people didn't exactly make it easy for him! But what Moses did get to experience in the wilderness was worth the hardship. Moses experienced God's presence. God was with him in the wilderness.

What do Exodus 33:11 and Deuteronomy 34:10 say about how Moses related to God?

Exodus 33:11 says the Lord spoke "to Moses face to face, as a man speaks to his friend." I don't know about you, but I can only imagine what that might be like. Yes, as a believer in Christ, I have received the Holy Spirit and can speak with the Lord whenever and wherever I am. I don't want to lose the awe and wonder of that reality. But to speak face-to-face? That will be something!

Record the promise found in 1 Corinthians 13:12.

Moses experienced an intimacy with the Lord we won't see this side of heaven, and yet, God's heart hasn't changed toward His people. The invitation to draw near to Him still stands. In the letter to the church in Laodicea, Jesus invites us to commune with Him. I love the New Living Translation of Revelation 3:20:

> *Look! I stand at the door and knock. If you hear my voice and open the door, I will come in, and we will share a meal together as friends.*

This appeal is extended to you too. Do you hear Him knocking? Will you open the door? Jesus doesn't care if you've tidied up or not. He simply desires to sit with you as you would sit with a dear friend over a meal together—all the laughter, all the tears, all the depth of conversation and communion.

What do you say to His offer? Write out a prayer, thanking Him for His presence and invitation.

DAY TWO
PEOPLE AND PLACE

Pause. Breathe. Pray.

Now that we have our bearings regarding where Numbers fits into God's redemptive story, it's time to home in on the book itself. There's no better place to start than at the beginning.

Write Numbers 1:1 below.

THE Lord SPOKE TO MOSES ... (NUM. 1:1).

Let's pick up where we left off yesterday: the incredibly mind-blowing notion that Moses spoke with the Lord as a man speaks with his friend. It wasn't always like this.

Read Exodus 3:1-6 and answer the following:

Where was Moses when God first spoke to him (v. 1)?

How did God appear to Moses (vv. 2,4)?

What instructions did God give Moses in approaching Him (v. 5)?

What was Moses' response (v. 6)?

I normally don't hide my face from my friends when they speak to me, but Moses had a good reason to hide his. His response reminds me of Isaiah's response to an encounter with our holy God.

In Isaiah 6 the prophet Isaiah received a vision of the Lord "sitting upon a throne, high and lifted up" (v. 1a). His robe filled the temple (v. 1b). Angels sang His praises so loudly that the foundations quaked (v. 4).

What words did Isaiah utter in response (v. 5)?

God's holy presence makes the true state of our souls crystal clear. Next to Him, even what we may see as our "smallest" sins are devastatingly dirty.

What's so startling about this scene is that when God called out to Moses from the bush, He summoned him with a "repetition of endearment." In Moses' culture, saying someone's name twice indicated affection and friendship.[3] The Lord beckoned Moses to come close, but not too close. We will see this theme repeated in God's interaction with His people and how He instructed them to arrange their camp.

IN THE WILDERNESS OF SINAI ... (NUM. 1:1).

We find Moses and the Israelites in the wilderness of Sinai. The Lord delivered them from slavery in Egypt and was leading them to the land He promised to Abraham and his descendants. The Hebrew word for *wilderness* is also interpreted as *desert*.[4] Instead of sand dunes and cacti, this kind is rocky with grazable grasses and small bushes. It's not a wholly hospitable land, but it's also not completely barren.

Remember how I told you that I love maps? I am welcoming you into my love by including one in the back of this study. When it's applicable, I will have you locate landmarks and trace Israel's route (as best we can) through the wilderness. Let's get started!

We will just get acquainted with the area this time. Locate the major regions and highlight or underline the following on page 224:
- **Egypt**
- **Canaan**
- **Midian**
- **Mount Sinai (circle)**
- **Sinai**
- **Moab**
- **Edom**

We see the wilderness theme repeated throughout Scripture. Often, the Lord leads His people into desolate places to invite them into a more intimate relationship with Him.

Look up these examples:

PERSON/ SCRIPTURE PASSAGE	SITUATION LEADING THIS PERSON INTO THE WILDERNESS	WHAT HAPPENED TO THIS PERSON IN THE WILDERNESS	HOW THIS PERSON LEFT THE WILDERNESS/ WHAT HAPPENED NEXT IN THIS PERSON'S LIFE
Hagar (Gen. 16:1-14)	Being mistreated by Sarai and Abram		
David (1 Sam. 21–23)			Eventually became king of Israel and a man after God's own heart.
Elijah (1 Kings 19:1-8)		God provided rest and sustenance for Elijah.	
Jesus (Matt. 4:1-11)			Jesus began His earthly ministry.

Can you think of any other examples of God using the wilderness to grow His people?

No matter how we get there, the wilderness is an opportunity to face our idols—the things or people we look to in place of God—confess our idolatry, cry out for God's rescue, repent from idolatry, receive His forgiveness, and walk humbly with Him.

When has God used the wilderness to teach you about Him?

IN THE TENT OF MEETING ... (NUM. 1:1).

The tent of meeting is also called the tabernacle. Moses received instruction from the Lord to take contributions from all the tribes of Israel to construct a sanctuary to be used to worship the Living God.

According to Exodus 25:8, why did the Lord want Moses to do this?

God's desire from the very beginning has been to dwell among His people. He walked in the garden with Adam and Eve (Gen. 3:8). He gave directions to Moses to build a tabernacle where He would dwell in their midst (Ex. 25:8). He sent His Son, Jesus, to dwell among humanity (John 1:14). After Jesus' death and resurrection, He promised the Holy Spirit as our Helper (John 16:7) who would dwell within us (1 Cor. 6:19). At the end of all things, in the new heaven and new earth, God's dwelling place will be with man (Rev. 21:3).

What do these verses reveal about God's heart toward His people?

Read below what the writer of Revelation (John) heard a loud voice saying in Revelation 21:3. Underline each time it says, "with man/them."

And I heard a loud voice from the throne saying,
"Behold, the dwelling place of God is with man. He
will dwell with them, and they will be his people, and
God himself will be with them as their God."

The tent of meeting is a shadow of God's ultimate goal for His people: that He would be with them as their God.

In the wilderness of Sinai, the presence of God is symbolized in two different forms. Look up Exodus 40:38 and record the two visual signals God gave to show His people He was in their midst.

In Exodus 40:34-35 was Moses able to enter the tabernacle? Why or why not?

In Leviticus 1:1 how did the Lord speak to Moses? (Hints: a preposition and a location!)

In light of those two texts, what is noteworthy about Numbers 1:1?

The fact that God spoke to Moses in the tent of meeting means that the Levitical law worked. Before the Israelites received instructions for how to approach God, the Lord spoke to Moses from the tent of meeting, not within it. But at the beginning of Numbers, God demonstrated how His plan to draw His people into a relationship with Him was possible.

> At the end of the previous book, Exodus, Moses, as Israel's representative, could not even enter God's presence in the tent. The Book of Leviticus opens by reminding us of this fundamental problem. It says, "the Lord called to Moses from the tent." So the question is, "How can Israel, in their sin and selfishness, be reconciled to this holy God?" That's what this book [Leviticus] is all about—how God is graciously providing a way for sinful, corrupt people to live in His holy presence. . . . Look at the first sentence of the next book of the Bible, Numbers. It begins, "The LORD spoke to Moses in the tent." So we can see that Moses is now able to enter God's presence on behalf of Israel. The Book of Leviticus—it worked! So despite Israel's failure, God has provided a way for their sin to be covered so that God can live with sinful people in peace.[5]

What does God's pattern of dwelling with His people reveal about His character?

What does His plan to dwell with you reveal about His thoughts toward you?

THE PEOPLE

Read Numbers 1:2-34.

According to Numbers 1:3, what requirements did the men have to meet in order to be included on Aaron's list?

This wasn't a general census. It was for military purposes. God was preparing His people to enter into the promised land by force.

List the tribes in the order they appear in Numbers 1:4-15. I've filled in a few for you. (Hint: "from" precedes each tribe.)

1. Reuben

2.

3.

4.

5.

6. Joseph/Ephraim

7. Joseph/Manasseh

8.

9.

10.

11.

12.

We should note a couple of items in this list. The first is that Joseph shared a place with Ephraim and Manasseh. What's going on there? At the end of his life, Israel adopted Joseph's sons Ephraim and Manasseh. He told Joseph they would be his sons like Reuben and Simeon were (Gen. 48:5). If you take a look back at the family tree in Day One's personal study (p. 15), you'll find a name is missing.

Who is missing from the list?

How does Numbers 1:47-49 account for this?

What were the Levites appointed to take care of (vv. 50-53)?

We find a significant sentence is at the end of chapter 1. Record Numbers 1:54 below.

You'll see in the rest of our study that this wasn't always the case. So let's put this in the praise column for Israel. The Israelites trusted God and obeyed Him—this time.

THE PLACE

Read Numbers 2.

In Numbers 2 we read that the Lord spoke to Moses and Aaron about the arrangement of camp. He was very specific in His organization of the tribes and the tabernacle. He even instructed the Israelites to camp "facing the tent of meeting on every side" (v. 2).

Using Numbers 2:1-31 as a reference, label the diagram of camp below.

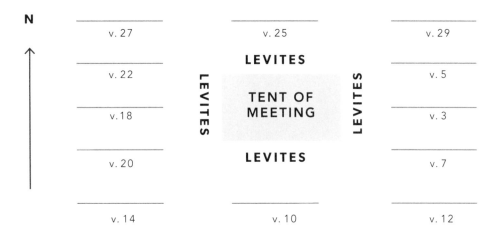

N

| v. 27 | v. 25 | v. 29 |

LEVITES

| v. 22 | | v. 5 |

LEVITES — TENT OF MEETING — LEVITES

| v.18 | | v. 3 |

| v. 20 | LEVITES | v. 7 |

| v. 14 | v. 10 | v. 12 |

We will get more specific tomorrow on the placement of the Levites, but for now, take a look at Israel's camp.

What do you think the arrangement of the tribes around the tabernacle implied?

Every tribe had a place in the camp. At its center was the presence of God— the tabernacle. Since each tent faced the tabernacle, God's people awoke and retired with the reality of the presence of God in their midst. Life is best lived with God in His proper place in our lives. As the planets revolve around the sun, and not vice versa, so our lives are made to revolve around the Lord. When we get this out of order, all manner of chaos ensues.

How have you seen this to be true in your own life? What happens when your life revolves around something (or someone) other than God?

If you were to draw a diagram of your life (and if you were gut-level honest), what would it look like? Who or what is at the center?

_____   _____   _____

_____   _____

_____   _____

_____   _____

_____   _____   _____

Father, thank You that You desire to dwell among Your people. Thank You for making that possible through Your Son, Jesus. Thank You that those who were far off may be brought near. Forgive us for putting ourselves, things, or people in Your rightful place. We invite You, God, to take Your place at the very center of our hearts. Amen.

DAY THREE
THE SONS OF LEVI

Pause. Breathe. Pray.

Read Numbers 3:1-39.

In chapter 3 the Lord turned His attention to the tribe of Levi. We saw in yesterday's personal study that they were excluded from the military census. The Levites were set apart and given special duties concerning the tabernacle and the people of Israel. But why the tribe of Levi? The answer to this question leads us to the first (of many) odd and violent stories in our study.

Exodus 32 describes the people of Israel as restless. Moses had been on Mount Sinai receiving the Law from God, but it took quite a bit longer than the Israelites anticipated. For forty days and forty nights, Moses was a no-show. At some point during this waiting, someone had the bright idea to ask Aaron (Moses' brother) to make gods for them. Aaron went with the crowd and took all their gold and fashioned a golden calf out of it. (In Aaron's version of the story, he took their gold, threw it in the fire, and out came this calf! Hmm—sounds a lot like a story my kids would tell.)

The Lord told Moses what happened and threatened to consume the people and start from scratch. Moses pleaded with the Lord to remember His covenant with Abraham and preserve the people, and the Lord relented. However, when Moses saw the debauchery with his own eyes, the mercy he previously had toward the people evaporated. He was so overwhelmed with anger that He threw down the tablets containing the Law, and they broke.

Read Exodus 32:26 and answer the following:

What question did Moses ask the people?

Who responded?

Moses then gave some pretty drastic instructions. Write down his words found in Exodus 32:27.

According to verse 28, who obeyed Moses' violent command?

What did Moses say to the sons of Levi in response (v. 29)?

The sons of Levi followed his orders. Moses said of them, "Today you have been ordained for the service of the LORD, each one at the cost of his son and of his brother, so that he might bestow a blessing upon you this day" (v. 29).

Did Moses forget commandment number six—"You shall not murder" (Ex. 20:13)? Surely not! So what could be going on here? We can tell from verses 30-33 that Levi's sons were not randomly killing people. Instead, they were carrying out the punishment for those who sinned against the Lord. The severity of the crime is reflected in the severity of the consequences. The people had sinned against a holy God. They had forsaken their Maker for what their hands had made.

It can be hard to reconcile what seems to be the harsh nature of God seen here with Jesus, who is called the Image of the Invisible God (Col. 1:15)—who laid down His life for His friends (John 15:13). But there is not a discrepancy like we might think at first glance. Jesus went on in John 15 to outline who His friends are—those who keep His commandments. He even said harder things than that.

Turn to the following texts and write the verses in the space provided:

MATTHEW 10:37

Isn't *hate* a rather bold word? What Jesus was saying here is that your love and devotion to Him must be so beyond the natural love you have for your family that it could almost be seen as hate in comparison. Before you give up hope (or throw this Bible study book against a wall), turn to 1 John 4:10 and write it below.

1 JOHN 4:10

Look up *propitiation* in a dictionary and write the definition here:

God knew we could not regain our favor or goodwill on our own. As we will clearly see in the Book of Numbers, humans are unable to keep the Law, so God made a way for us through His Son.

Philippians 2:8 says, ". . . he humbled himself by becoming obedient to the point of death, even death on a cross." The bloodbath at Calvary displayed the depth of our sin and the depths to which God would go to save us and make good on His promise to Abraham that all the peoples of the earth would be blessed.

We will need to hold the tension that the God of the Old Testament is indeed the God of the New. He hasn't and won't change. God is love. Because He loves us, He will not put up with lesser loves or gods in our hearts. Jesus gave His all so that He would have our all.

The Levites proved they were willing to obey God even at a personal cost. Because of this, God gave them the privilege and duty to take care of and guard the tabernacle and its furnishings.

THE SONS OF AARON

Remember, what was Moses' relationship to Aaron?

According to Exodus 6:25-26, what tribe were Moses and Aaron from?

Aaron was Moses' brother and a Levite. God appointed Aaron and his sons to be priests, the most holy of the families of Levi. They were set apart to minister before the Lord in the Holy Place inside the tabernacle, making sacrifices and offerings according to the Law.

Refer to Numbers 3:2-4 and list Aaron's sons. Note anything exceptional about them.

1.

2.

3.

4.

We find the story of Nadab and Abihu's demise in Leviticus 10:1-3. It's not entirely clear what was "unauthorized" about the fire they offered, but it's safe to assume it was not according to God's Law. Again, we see how serious the Lord is about obedience, especially when it comes to approaching a holy God.

DUTIES OF THE LEVITES

Read Numbers 3:40-51.

Aaron and his sons were tasked with the important (and dangerous) job of guarding the tabernacle itself and packing up the furnishings and items inside according to the Lord's specific directions. The rest of the Levites were given two jobs: (1) Guard the tabernacle from intruders and (2) take care of and transport the tabernacle and its furnishings. God gave specific tasks to specific clans. And, just as He designated places around the tabernacle for the other tribes, He gave these clans similar instructions.

Refer to Numbers 3:21-39 to complete the diagram below.

CLAN:

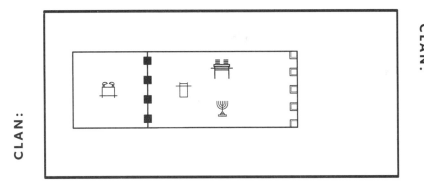

CLAN:

CLAN:

CLAN:

Numbers 3 and 4 record two censuses of the Levites.

Census One:
• recorded in Numbers 3:15-39;
• counted every male one month and older;
• the total number was twenty-two thousand.

The purpose of this census was for the redemption of the firstborn from among the other tribes. When Israel was delivered out of slavery, the last plague to befall Egypt before Israel's flight was the death of every firstborn male—human and cattle. God gave instructions to His people that would protect them from this plague. In Exodus 13:2 God told Moses: "Consecrate to me all the firstborn. Whatever is the first to open the womb among the people of Israel, both of man and of beast, is mine."

In Numbers the "male Levites took the place of the firstborn males of the other tribes in order to serve the Lord, so the first census ensured that the number of the former matched the number of the latter."[6]

Read Numbers 4.

Census Two:
- **What were the age requirements for the men listed in the second census (vv. 3,23,30,35,39,43,47)?**

- **What was the total number (v. 48)?**

List the work each clan was required to do.

Kohathites (v. 15):

Gershonites (vv. 25-26):

Merarites (vv. 31-32):

Each clan's responsibility had a theme. The Kohathites guarded and carried the items within the tabernacle; the Gershonites guarded and carried what made up the outside of the tabernacle, and the Merarites guarded and carried the structural components of the tabernacle. Since these items were quite heavy, able-bodied men were needed to carry them, thus the age requirement of thirty to fifty years.

In Numbers 4:17-20 God warned His people to take His holiness seriously. Although the Kohathites were tasked to carry the holy things, they were not priests and thus were not allowed to look upon them "even for a moment, lest they die" (v. 20).

God didn't wish for these men to die. That's why He strongly charged Moses and Aaron to not let the Kohathites go near the most holy things before they were properly wrapped.

We can't let the severe consequences of approaching a holy God in haste obscure God's goal. He is the Lord who desires to dwell among His people. In order for Him to do so, He must establish boundaries and processes for His sin-sick children to draw near to Him. For the children of Israel in Numbers, it was living according to the Law with its offerings and sacrifices that ultimately point to the perfect life, offering, and sacrifice of Jesus. As believers in Christ, we get to approach the throne of grace with confidence because Jesus has gone before us (Heb. 4:16). Jesus is our High Priest (like Aaron, but so much better!) who enters in on our behalf so we might draw near to God and He to us.

We also can't forget the camping and traveling arrangements were temporary. God was taking His children somewhere. Before they arrived, He was preparing them to live in the land He provided. The wilderness was not haphazard nor wasted. God had delivered His children out of Egypt, but it was time to deliver Egypt out of them.

> **If you're in a wilderness season (or have experienced one), does (or did) it feel haphazard? Why or why not? Reflect on a wilderness season in your own life. Did it feel wasted at the time?**

> **How do you want to respond to God's invitation to draw near to Him? Do you have confidence to do so after? Why or why not?**

Father, thank You that You never waste a season. Jesus, thank You for making a way for us to draw near to the Father. Holy Spirit, help us to respond to Your tender conviction of sin and assure us of our acceptance through Jesus' blood. Amen.

DAY FOUR
CLEANSING THE CAMP

Pause. Breathe. Pray.

Read Numbers 5.

Today's text isn't likely to be the most popular for devotional reading, but my prayer is that you would see God's consistent character and be comforted that He never changes. He is consistently holy and compassionate, just and merciful. When everything else seems to change, He alone remains.

UNCLEAN

Look at Numbers 5:1-4 and answer the following questions:

What three groups of people were to be put out of camp?

According to verse 3, why were they put out of camp?

God was preparing His people to march into the promised land. The only real shot they had was to enter with the Lord in their midst. Without Him, it couldn't happen. Because God is holy, in order for Him to remain in their midst, they had to be consecrated.

Look up *consecrate* in a dictionary. Write the definition that best fits below:

Write out Leviticus 20:7-8.

The Lord is serious about holiness and thus "clean-ness." He told His children what was clean and unclean, acceptable and unacceptable among His people. Sometimes a person is unclean due to personal sin (e.g. sexual immorality, idolatry, and murder), but other times, it's something over which they have little control. This was the case with the three groups of people listed at the beginning of chapter 5.

Their uncleanness was communicable and posed a threat to the sanctity of the camp. If the camp was defiled, there was a greater risk the tabernacle would be defiled as well.

In the New Testament, we see God is still serious about holiness. The apostle Peter urged Christians to "be holy in all your conduct, since it is written, 'You shall be holy, for I am holy'" (1 Pet. 1:15b-16). In Revelation 21 we see that the new Jerusalem (where God dwells with His people) will have no place for death or anything unclean.

The *Tyndale Old Testament Commentary* states:

> But if the New Testament upholds the moral side of these uncleanness regulations, it abolished the symbolic physical distinctions. Our Lord healed lepers and the woman with a flow of blood, and raised the dead through touch (Lk. 17:12ff.; 8:40ff.). In these ways he declared that those conditions which for centuries had separated even the elect people of God from God no longer mattered. God has himself drawn nigh. The kingdom of heaven is now open to all who repent and believe the gospel.[7]

While these regulations were appropriate for God's people in Numbers, they are no longer relevant for those who trust in Christ. Jesus has made us clean through His blood. It is His touch that makes us clean.

RESTITUTION

Numbers 5:5-10 addresses moral "uncleanness," focusing on a man or woman who had sinned against another (most likely they had stolen or damaged someone else's property).[8] Notice, though, that the Lord referred to their sin as "breaking faith with the LORD" (v. 5). Our sin against one another is ultimately sin against God.

Turn to Matthew 22:34-40 and answer the following questions:

Who asked Jesus a question?

What is the first and greatest commandment?

What is the second that is like the first?

The lawyer in Matthew 22 was not legal counsel in a court of federal or state law; he was an expert in the Law of God. He knew all the commandments and the requirements for offerings, sacrifices, feasts, and fasts. Because we know this, it is safe to assume he wasn't asking Jesus the question to get information. He was testing Jesus. True to form, Jesus was undeterred. He answered clearly, acknowledging that loving the Lord your God is connected with loving your neighbor and reiterating that sinning against one's neighbor is breaking faith with the Lord.

The Lord knew that sinning against a brother or sister would be a reality of life, and He made a way for His people to make things right. In Numbers God provided a way through confession, restitution, and the offering of a ram. In the New Testament and for us, Jesus became our *propitiation* (there's that word again!).

Compare Matthew 5:23-26 and Matthew 6:14-15.

What did Jesus instruct us to do when we sin against someone? When someone sins against us?

Whether we mean to or not, we will hurt others, and we will be hurt by others. When we do, we have the choice to confess our wrong or to justify and shift blame. Will we extend forgiveness, or will we dwell on the hurt and demand revenge? As Christians, we know we cannot live this life perfectly; thus, we are free to admit our sins and receive forgiveness. And since we have been so freely forgiven by God, we can forgive others. Forgiveness is not an easy process. It doesn't always mean restoration of a relationship, but it does mean freedom for the forgiver.

For me, forgiveness for someone who had hurt me was a longer process than I thought it would be. First, I didn't realize I harbored unforgiveness toward that person. It only became evident when I found bitterness leaking into my thoughts and comments about that person. My gut reaction was to justify my feelings—after all, I was legitimately hurt. However, the Lord would not let up with His gentle reminder, *Lauren, you need to deal with this. Forgive that person.* I started out listing the ways I felt wronged to the Lord. Then, I asked Him to forgive me for holding on to bitterness. I surrendered any right I thought I had to "punish" that person. I put it in the Lord's hands alone.

Finally, I got to the place where I spoke the words, "I forgive _____ for _____." Then, I asked the Lord to help me live the forgiveness I had spoken. I prayed the Lord would bless him/her and specifically listed out ways He might do this. Now, I didn't magically feel affection or tenderness toward that person (but anything is possible with God!), nor did I stop feeling a little stab of pain when his/her name was mentioned or when I saw him/her. But the pain has lessened as I have reminded myself that I have laid my hurt down and picked up the forgiveness Jesus offers me and the one who wounded me. That is where I have found freedom.

Do you have something for which you need to ask forgiveness from someone? Will you have the courage to put feet to that? Make a plan to do so.

Do you need to forgive someone? If so, who and for what?

If there's someone you need to forgive, be encouraged that this may be a long process, but the first step is acknowledging the unforgiveness and confessing it as sin to the Lord. From there, trust the Lord, ask Him to help you turn from your bitterness and forgive like He has. Walk in the forgiveness you've received from God and ask Him to help you extend it to others.

THE ORDEAL OF JEALOUSY

Read Numbers 5:11-31.

Now we come to another strange text. I know y'all are chomping at the bit to talk about the spirit of jealousy, drinking dusty water, thighs falling away, and bellies swelling. Before we start, let's chat about Western minds. (I'm not referring to cowboy hats and horses, but minds shaped by the Enlightenment.) Western minds like dealing with facts and reality. We're not much for imagination (unless it's for innovation). Eastern minds (the perspective from which the biblical writers viewed the world) value imagery and ritual.[9] We see that value in this section.

What were the circumstances that called for this "test" (vv. 11-15)?

What offering was required of her (v. 15)?

According to Leviticus 2:1-2, of what did the grain offering usually comprise? What's different in Numbers 5?

What was the woman given to drink? What would be its effect (vv. 16-22)?

This ceremony was a sad occasion. At best, it showed that a spirit of jealousy had come over a man; he didn't trust his wife. Trust lost is a painful thing. At worst, it proved the breaking of the covenant between a man and a woman and caused suffering for both. The usual grain offering included oil and frankincense which symbolized joy and the Spirit of God. Both of these were missing from this particular offering. Unbinding the woman's hair was considered shameful.[10] There she was, naked, in a sense, before the Lord. The holy water mixed with dust from the floor of the tabernacle would have been disastrous to drink if she were guilty. Because of her uncleanness, she could have died taking in the holy water. And if she didn't die, she would become barren. Her sin would be manifest, and her life would be forever changed.

The ancient Near East was an especially cruel place and time to be a woman. Women had little protection. The strong overpowered the weak. While there are a few exceptions of physically stout women, for the most part, men are physically stronger. And at this point in history, men had all the cultural power as well. It would not have been out of the ordinary for a man to simply act on a suspicion and cast his wife aside. Not so for the people of Israel. The Lord set them apart by requiring this strange-to-us test. If the woman was innocent, the Lord provided an opportunity for her to be vindicated. If she was guilty, the consequences upheld God's high standard for marriage.

Marriage was (and still is) a picture of God's love for His people. To break faith in marriage is to break faith with God. Time and again, Old Testament prophets used the language of marriage to describe Israel's rebellion and idolatry. They were adulterers and harlots who chose another lover over their husband. The uncleanness of adultery could not be tolerated within the camp.

For believers today, we see that God is still serious about marriage and preserving its purity. Jesus took it a step further in Matthew 5 by saying that even lusting in one's heart is the same as committing adultery (v. 28). But He also makes a way for the adulterer who is repentant.

Turn to 1 John 1:9 and write it here.

Is there something for you to confess? Something hidden? Sin against a brother or sister? Unforgiveness? Unfaithfulness? Use this time and space to confess and receive God's forgiveness and cleansing. If appropriate, find someone you trust to share this with who can help you walk in the light.

DAY FIVE
A VOW + A BLESSING

Pause. Breathe. Pray.

Read Numbers 6.

Who could make a Nazirite vow?

What was the purpose of the Nazirite vow?

In the table below, list what the Nazirite was separated from and to:

SEPARATED FROM	SEPARATED TO

The Nazirite vow was a serious promise and dedication to God that any layperson, male or female, could make. Most vows only lasted for a specific amount of time, but Scripture has examples of those whose vows lasted a lifetime. For instance, Samson, Samuel, and John the Baptist were lifelong Nazirites.

It makes sense that the guidelines for this vow are listed immediately after the cleansing of the camp. The Nazirite vow is a radical picture of Israel's consecration and dedication to the Lord. Those taking the vow were to be separated from wine, wine vinegar, strong drink, and pretty much anything to do with grapes. They were to let their hair grow as a sign of their dedication. The *ESV Study Bible's* notes on Numbers 6:7 highlight the connection between the Nazirite's uncut hair and Israel's calling.

> The word here translated "separation" (Hb. *nezer*) is also used of the high priest's crown (Lev. 8:9). Both the priestly crown and the Nazirite's uncut hair reminded other people of their dedication to God's service. In this way the dedication of the Nazirites was a challenge to every Israelite to follow the Lord wholeheartedly.[11]

They also could not be near death, including the death of a relative or even someone who happened to drop dead next to them. If the latter occurred, they had to shave their hair, make a sin offering, and start the vow all over. Here again, we see God's utter displeasure and incompatibility with death.

Since we believe Jesus is fully God, and in light of His relationship with death, how incredible is it that Jesus endured the most violent, humiliating, and unclean death on the cross?

Vows like the Nazirite vows are no longer necessary for the Christian, but we can still see vestiges of the practice today. Nuns and monks take vows to the Lord to dedicate their entire lives of service to Him. Their devotion is inspiring. Even the apostle Paul commended a set apart lifestyle (1 Cor. 7:1-7). Though not all are called to live set apart in these ways, all of Christ's followers are called to live with integrity.

What "set apart" choice do Matthew 5:37 and James 5:12 ask us to make?

How well do you let your yes be yes and your no be no?

How could you grow in this?

Sometimes our yeses and noes lie outside of our control. Other times, we fail to keep our promises. In that case, we can acknowledge and ask forgiveness for our failures. In both cases, we can rest in the integrity and faithfulness of God.

THE PRIESTLY BLESSING

This section of laws and cleansing requirements closes with a poem of benediction. If you've spent any time in church, it is likely you have heard the Aaronic blessing.

Write the blessing found in Numbers 6:24-26 below.

Circle "the LORD" each time it occurs.

Underline the verbs (what "the LORD" will do for and toward Israel).

This blessing is probably one of the oldest poems in Scripture. The repetition of "the LORD" at the beginning of each line emphasizes the only possible source and sustenance for such blessing. In the Old Testament, *bless* has a very specific meaning. The Lord "blesses people by giving them children, property, land, good health, and his presence (Gen. 17:16; 22:17f; Lev. 26:3-13; Deut. 28:2-14)." The Lord "keeps" His people by guarding and protecting them. For God to "shine his face" on them is to liken Him to the favor and grace sunshine brings. A shining face is a smiling face. Lifting up His countenance means to take notice of a person and treat them specially. The peace that is mentioned here is the Hebrew word *shalom*. It isn't just peace in wartime, but wholeness and well-being. It is the "sum total of all God's good gifts to his people."[12]

List some of the blessings God has given you.

Read Psalms 67 and 121 and note the echoes of the Aaronic blessing. Write down ideas that are repeated.

This blessing is still appropriate for God's people to speak over one another. I have an exercise for you to practice.

If you are in a group Bible study, take a moment when you gather to speak this blessing over one another. If you are alone, find someone to speak it over and have them speak it over you.

What parts of the blessing were easy for you to receive? What parts were hard?

To close, read Ephesians 2:14-22 and ask the Lord to help you receive His blessing.

Only through Jesus are we able to truly have peace with God and others. He gives peace, made peace through His sacrifice on the cross, and continues to be our Peace.

Write a prayer of response to His blessing and peace.

I've provided some discussion questions here to get the conversation started. Feel free to discuss what you learned throughout the week of study, ask any questions you may have, and share what God is teaching you.

DISCUSSION QUESTIONS

Which story about the "colorful cast of characters" that you read about this week stuck with you the most? Why?

God often uses wilderness seasons to remind you that life is best when centered on Him. Talk through that idea in your group together. What might that look like practically in your life?

For those who are comfortable, take a few moments to discuss the diagram of your life and what it's centered on (at the end of Day Two, p. 28). What do you notice about the things you're centering your life on? Does anything need to change?

Our God-centered lives are meant to be a blessing to those around us. Discuss with your group ways that you might care for others with the overflow of God's care in your life. With people in your everyday lives—family and friends? With your larger sphere of influence?

Him at the Center of it All

Teaching sessions available for purchase or rent at *LifeWay.com/WithUsInTheWilderness*

Is God the Center?
Or am I the center
or someone/something else?

Big Bold God
in the Center

When our lives are centered on and around God, our lives work and it spills over - when we believe we are blessed, beloved children of God.

COMMUNITY AND CONFLICT

At the command of the LORD they camped,
and at the command of the LORD they set
out. They kept the charge of the LORD, at
the command of the LORD by Moses.

NUMBERS 9:23

GENEROUS GOD, GENEROUS RESPONSE

Pause. Breathe. Pray.

Welcome to a new week in the wilderness! Last session's passage set the stage for the people of Israel to start their journey toward the promised land. The people were counted; men able to fight were identified; the camp was arranged; tasks were assigned to the Levites and priests; instructions for keeping the camp clean were given; a blessing was spoken over the people.

What more could there be to do?

> **Read Numbers 7 quickly all the way through. (You'll notice a little repetition. Don't worry about reading carefully right now; we'll look at the verses more closely as we study.)**

> **When did all the chiefs bring their offerings to the tabernacle (vv. 1-2)?**

> **When was the tabernacle erected? (See Ex. 40:2.)**

> **When does Numbers 1 pick up in the narrative (v. 1)?**

> **Why do you think this narrative (Num. 7) was placed out of chronological order?**

Now, turn your attention from *when* this happened to the *what*. (I won't leave you hanging on the question above. Hold tight. I'll get there!)

What did Moses do to the tabernacle's furnishings, altar, and utensils?

Anoint and *consecrate* can feel like antiquated church words, causing us to rush right past them and miss the significance of what is being described in these verses.

God often commanded *anointing* in the Book of Exodus (and throughout the rest of Scripture). The following verses describe the practice. Jot down what anointing involved in each verse.

EXODUS 29:7

EXODUS 29:21

EXODUS 30:29-31

Consecrate means to declare something as sacred.[1] Moses placed oil on the tabernacle furnishings and altar as a way of expressing their hallowed significance.

In Numbers 7:2-3 who brought their offerings to the Lord?

List any details recorded about the offerings.

Record how many oxen and wagons were given to the Gershonites and the Merarites.

Gershonites: _____ wagons and _____ oxen (v. 7).

Merarites: _____ wagons and _____ oxen (v. 8).

Think (or turn) back to Day Three of last session's personal study (p. 29). Why would Moses give these specific amounts to these specific Levites?

What reason does Numbers 7:9 give for Moses refraining from giving wagons and oxen to the Kohathites?

All of the details of these offerings can feel tedious to us and may have felt tedious to the Israelites too.

In what ways have God's commands felt tedious in your own life?

THE TWELVE DAYS OF OFFERINGS

As I write this study, the holiday season is quickly approaching. Members of our church's worship team gather in early December to eat sweets, sip cider, and, of course, sing carols. The most requested song is always "The Twelve Days of Christmas." My theory is that by the time you get to the very end, you're either delirious or so tickled at the monotony that every syllable is dramatically extended to a hilarious degree. No matter how many carolers sputter out of steam at "ten lords a-leaping," everyone rallies for the "twelve drummers drumming."

Maybe you can identify with this delirium because (a) you've participated in this sort of sing-along, or (b) you followed my instructions and read all of Numbers 7, or (c) all of the above. We'll play our own version, "The Twelve Days of Offerings," in the table on the next page!

Use Numbers 7:12-83 as a guide to fill out the chart.

DAY	CHIEF/PRINCE	TRIBE	ITEMS BOUGHT BY THE CHIEF	WHICH OFFERINGS THE ITEMS WERE USED FOR (IF INDICATED)
1				
2				
3				
4				
5				
6				
7				
8				
9				
10				
11				
12				

Every offering the chiefs brought to the tabernacle enabled the priests to carry out their duties. Without the offerings, the priests could not honor God's commanded rituals. Without the priests, no one could make the offerings. This was an all-hands-on-deck situation. Although the chiefs brought the offerings, it was not they alone who raised the livestock, ground grain into fine flour, or gave up expensive oil. The weight of God's law didn't just fall on the chiefs and the priests; everyone felt it.

The ministry and sacrifices involved in worshiping God in the wilderness of Sinai are not unlike those in the life of the New Testament believer. While Christians do not have to bring bulls, goats, pigeons, or grain to worship or make atonement for sin, we still respond to God's grace in worship through the sacrifice of our own comforts and selves in order to honor God and share the gospel (Rom. 12:1; 1 Cor. 9:3-27).

> **According to Hebrews 10:11-14, why do Christians no longer need to offer the types of sacrifices and offerings found in the Old Testament?**

> **What should our sacrifices and offerings look like today? (See Rom. 12:1 and 1 Cor. 9:13-14.)**

A GENEROUS RESPONSE TO A GENEROUS BLESSING

We can only guess why the account of the consecration of the tabernacle was placed in Numbers 7 instead of Exodus 40 when the tabernacle was originally built, but what we can know with certainty is that it wasn't by mistake. Although there are various reasons why it makes sense thematically, the fact that it follows the Aaronic blessing (Num. 6:22-27) shows that God's people responded to His gracious blessing with gratitude and generosity.

In 2009 my husband, Matt, was diagnosed with a malignant brain tumor. He had surgery to remove the tumor and radiation and chemotherapy to destroy any remaining cancerous cells. It was a tumultuous time for our family to say the least. The generosity of our church and community was overwhelming. They provided meals, gifts for our kids, a spa day for me, and nonstop prayers for Matt's full recovery. I remember wanting to make sure someone else felt that in their season of need. While my gratitude and generosity have taken many forms since then, one of the small ways I expressed it during that time was by always giving a cash donation when asked for one at the checkout line in the grocery store. I know it's just a little thing in light of the huge blessing we received, but it was something. And I was grateful.

Can you think of a time when someone's generosity to you has led you to be generous to others? If so, describe it.

How has the Lord been generous to you? Make a list.

Has the Lord's generosity to you led you to gratitude and generosity? How has that worked itself out in your life?

Our generosity is always a response to God's generosity (whether we know it or not). God is generous to give us life, breath, the ability to behold a sunset, and to enjoy a good meal. He is generous to give us His Son, Jesus, for the forgiveness of our sins and communion with the Living God. Even in the wilderness, we have something to be grateful for and thus, an opportunity for generosity. In response, we can thank Him for His presence and give our lives as an offering.

What are ways you can be generous both to God and to others this week? Make a plan to put a few of these ideas into action.

Look at Numbers 7:89. How does this chapter end?

The twelve days of offerings were not in vain. Their generous group effort resulted in Moses going before the Lord on behalf of the people and hearing His voice. But now, with the completion of the tabernacle and the twelve days of consecration, Yahweh met with Moses in the midst of His people, revealing

Himself in a new setting. The ultimate fulfillment and demonstration of this image was expressed by the apostle John when he declared: "The Word became flesh and made his dwelling among us. We have seen his glory, the glory of the one and only Son, who came from the Father, full of grace and truth" (John 1:14, NIV).

The word translated *made his dwelling* or *dwelt* is also the word used for *tabernacle*.[2]

> Knowing what you know now about the tabernacle and its purpose, what does this verse tell you about the character of God?

> How does knowing that Jesus "tabernacled" among us lead you to worship? Write out a prayer of thanksgiving and praise to Him.

DAY TWO
LAMPS AND LEVITES

Pause. Breathe. Pray.

When my kids were younger, it never failed that as we headed out the door, someone could not find his or her shoes. No matter how many times that happened, I rarely built in space for a shoe hunt, thus we were perpetually late to almost every play date or appointment. While I miss much about that season of life, I don't miss the curious case of the missing shoes.

Everyone in Numbers 8 seemed to be able to locate their shoes, but their departure was still delayed. A few more things had to be done before they moved on.

> Go ahead and read the entire chapter of Numbers 8. (Don't worry: it's not nearly as long or as repetitive as chapter 7!) Note anything that stands out to you.

LAMPS AND THE LAMPSTAND

At the close of Numbers 7, we saw that Moses was able to enter the tabernacle and hear the voice of the Lord. The Hebrew verb translated as *speaking* here implies a conversational sort of interaction.[3] It's not one-sided. Moses was conversing with God.

> How does God speak to us today? How have you experienced conversation with Him?

I pray that we never lose the awe of being able to interact with the Living God through His Word and the Holy Spirit residing in us!

> What was the first thing the Lord told Moses in Numbers 8:2?

We are going to do a little artistic exercise here. I'm sure some of y'all are chomping at the bit while others might be tempted to skip this part. Don't! We get to put ourselves in Moses' shoes and "construct" the lampstand (also called a menorah) with its lamps as instructed by the Lord in Exodus 25.

Refer to Exodus 25:31-40 and draw what the Lord described. Feel free to look up what an almond blossom looks like, what a calyx is, or anything that might help you figure this out. However, try to follow the instructions in Exodus more than copying what you find online. (One hint: think of a genie's lamp for the *lamps* as opposed to candles.)

Now, there's no judgment in drawing skills, nor in interpreting the Lord's pattern for the lampstand to Moses. To be fair, the Lord showed Moses what it would look like on the mountain (v. 40).

What does the lampstand remind you of?

If you answered *tree*, is there a tree (or trees) in Scripture that comes to mind?

Everything about the tabernacle, its furnishings, and utensils were meant to be a replica of a heavenly reality—God's sanctuary in heaven. Its design also had another purpose.

As many scholars have acknowledged, the tabernacle/temple was planned and designed to remind worshipers of the garden in Eden as a sanctuary with Adam as its priest. In the midst of the garden-sanctuary was the tree of life. The menorah was symbolic not only of life, but of eternal life for the true people of God. It not only looked back to the tree of life in the garden, but it also anticipated the tree of life that stands in the new heavens and the new earth in Revelation 22.[4]

The lampstand represented life and light that God offers to His people. As Christians, we no longer need lamps in order to worship the Lord. When Jesus came, He announced, "I am the light of the world. Whoever follows me will not walk in darkness, but will have the light of life" (John 8:12).

Even as little children, we know darkness isn't a good thing. We fear what it covers up—the unknown monsters in the closet or lurking under our beds. Because of sin, our hearts are darkened and our understanding of God, ourselves, and others is skewed. We need the light of Christ to show us who God is and who we are. So God gave us Jesus as the Word (John 1:1)—the truest Image of God (Col. 1:15)—the radiance of His glory and the exact imprint of His nature (Heb. 1:3). We look to Him, and we see what God is like. He also gave us His Word, to be a lamp to our feet and a light to our path (Ps. 119:105), to show us the Way, Jesus (John 14:6), and to discern the thoughts and intentions of our hearts (Heb. 4:12).

Record Leviticus 24:2 below.

The lamps sat on top of the seven branches of the lampstand. So it makes sense that Aaron could turn them to give light in front of the lampstand. This action enabled the light to shine directly upon the table of showbread, "the bread of the Presence" (Ex. 25:30) and also illuminate the altar of incense.

According to Leviticus 24:5-9, what was the bread of the Presence?

How often was it to be replaced?

Who replaced it?

The bread of the Presence was meant to be a reminder of God's provision for His people. The twelve loaves hinted at the twelve tribes of Israel. Gordon J. Wenham explains that the arrangement of the lampstand shining its light toward the table containing the bread of the Presence "portrayed visually God's intention that his people should live continually in his presence and enjoy the blessing mediated by his priests."[5]

We don't have to have a high priest like Aaron to mediate for us anymore. Instead, we have a better Aaron in Jesus who is at the right hand of God and is perpetually interceding for us (Rom. 8:34). When Jesus ascended into heaven to sit at God's right hand, He didn't leave us alone. He sent the Holy Spirit to help us. Our bodies became temples of the Holy Spirit (1 Cor. 6:19). His presence is with us and, mysteriously, in us (Col. 1:27).

Where are you most attuned to the reality of God's presence? Take a moment to thank Him for that space or place.

THE CLEANSING OF THE LEVITES

Numbers 8 moves on to the cleansing of the Levites for the bulk of the chapter. Just as the camp was required to be cleansed, the Levites, who carried the weight (literally and figuratively) of the duties pertaining to the tabernacle, needed cleansing.

How were the Levites cleansed physically (v. 7)?

Describe what happened next (vv. 8-13).

Remember, at the end of Numbers 3 the Levites were substituted for all the firstborn sons of Israel. The act of the people placing their hands on the heads of the Levites symbolized the substitution. The Levites, in turn, laid their hands on the heads of the bulls to make atonement for their sins. They had been made physically clean, and now, they were made spiritually clean in the eyes of God.

The end of Numbers 8 records the age limits for the Levites' service in the tabernacle.

At what age did the Levites begin their terms of service (v. 24)?

At what age were the Levites required to withdraw from duty (v. 25)?

Compare this with Numbers 4:23. What difference do you see?

We aren't entirely sure what accounts for the discrepancy in the required ages of the Levites, but John D. Currid notes that "The rabbis answer the dilemma by saying that the Levites start their training at the age of twenty-five, but do not enter into full-time duty until they are thirty."[6]

Humor me for a bit as I take us on a slight rabbit trail. In our fast-paced, instantly gratified culture, apprenticeship has lost its allure. We want it all now—the experience, the respect, the seat at the table. But there is wisdom in waiting and watching someone else do the work and enjoy the spotlight. Perhaps by watching them in the spotlight, we realize the work is much harder than we thought, and the fruit of the labor satisfying in an entirely different way.

Have you experienced this? From which perspective—the apprentice or the one in the spotlight? Briefly describe.

Considering all we've learned so far about what was required for service in the temple, why do you think an apprenticeship of sorts may have been needed?

While we may tend to skip over these sections of Scripture, thinking they don't apply to our lives today, I hope learning more about the Levites helped demonstrate God's intentionality with His people.

PASSOVER, PRESENCE, AND PASSAGE

Pause. Breathe. Pray.

We are hardwired for traditions. When I was thirteen or fourteen, my family decided to go skiing over Christmas break. Growing up in Texas, we rarely (if ever) experienced a white Christmas. This year would be different. We would cozy up by a crackling fire, hot cocoa in hand, as we each gazed out the window that framed a picture-perfect winter wonderland. We arrived a few days before Christmas to ski and play in the snow. We even scouted a Charlie Brown® evergreen to adorn with popcorn garlands and one string of multicolored lights from the grocery store. We hung stockings, donned the tree, and tucked ourselves in on Christmas Eve. On Christmas morning, we woke to carols playing on the radio and a fire in the hearth. We opened presents one by one. (There's no all-at-once in the Walker home. We share the joy of each person's gift as they open it.) We read the story of the first Christmas found in Matthew. While our location and scenery had changed, our traditions had not, making the little condo tucked into the New Mexico mountains feel a little more like home.

Do you or your family have traditions especially dear to you? What are they?

Read Numbers 9:1-14. What's the "date" for this passage (hint: verse 1)?

Did you notice a phrase and/or word that is repeated frequently in this passage? If so, which one?

I recently watched an illusionist on television approach total strangers and ask them to think of any celebrity, and he would write their answers (before they gave them) on a dry-erase board. Each time he turned the board to face the participant with the celebrity's name written on it, the participant was in complete awe. He then proceeded to share with the viewers that every person he approached had the same answer. How could this be? They rewound the tape to the conversations he had with each person before he asked the question and prior to the clip the viewers had previously seen. He dropped seemingly subtle hints by working into the casual conversation several movie titles that featured the celebrity. Subliminal messaging is real!

A form of the words *keep, observe,* or *celebrate* appears twelve times in Numbers 9:1-14! Do you think He was trying to get a point across to His people here? The Lord knew His people were prone to forget, so He established traditions for them and utilized repetition to help them remember.

THE PASSOVER

We find the first Passover in Exodus 12. The Lord was about to deliver Israel from the clutches of Egypt through Moses. Egypt had already endured nine plagues. With each plague the Egyptians suffered, Israel was immune. But with the tenth and final plague, God's people were required to follow God's instructions so their homes would be "passed over" (v. 27) and untouched by the effects of this final, most devastating plague.

> **Read Exodus 12:1-13 and answer the following questions:**
>
> **What animal was taken for each household? (Include its required attributes.)**
>
>
>
> **After the animals were killed, what were God's people instructed to do with it?**
>
>
>
> **In what manner were they to eat it (v. 11)?**

What did the Lord say would be a sign for them? What would He do in response to the sign?

In Exodus 12:14-20 the Lord declared that the Passover would be a memorial day for them. All the Israelites were to keep Passover every year as a feast to the Lord and "as a statute forever" (v. 14).

Define *statute*:

Before the people of Israel set out toward the wilderness from Egypt, they observed the Passover. Here again, in Numbers 9, the people were set to move toward the promised land, one year from their deliverance. In the Lord's kindness, He didn't just sit back and wait to see if they remembered. Instead, He spoke to Moses and reminded him of the statute He had ordained.

Why do you think it was important for the Israelites to remember the Passover, especially as they set out again?

We are prone to historical revisionism. We can forget details or give credit where it doesn't belong or blame where there is none. Personally, I can look back on an event and overestimate my contribution. I can pat myself on the back for a job well done when, in fact, while I may have been obedient, the credit belongs to God. Maybe it was a stellar parenting moment or a powerful time of worship in which I got to lead. My obedience may be commended, but it was simply the Holy Spirit's fruit in the moment.

I can imagine the people of Israel might relate. They'd had their bouts with forgetfulness. The Red Sea parted before their eyes. They walked on dry land with water piled up on either side. But as soon as Moses was MIA, they ditched the Lord and fashioned their own god. Maybe they started to think exiting Egypt was their idea. Maybe they believed their might delivered them from Egypt's armies. The Passover begged to differ. It reminded them that the Lord supernaturally rescued them from their oppressors. If He did it then, surely He could do it again, in the midst of the wilderness and as they settled in the promised land.

Can you think of a time the Lord came through for you in a way that was indisputable?

Even when we've seen Him come through for us time and time again, we can still doubt He'll come through for us the next time.

Do you ever doubt that God will keep His promises? What Scripture or attribute of God comes to mind to help you overcome that doubt?

PROVISIONS

According to Numbers 9:6-14, what two groups did the Lord make special provisions for in keeping the Passover?

Who was without excuse for not keeping the Passover?

What happened to someone who failed to observe the Passover but wasn't a part of one of these two groups (v. 13)?

What do these laws tell you about the importance of Passover?

What do they tell you about the character of God?

The Lord is not unreasonable. He gave provisions for those who were unable to keep the Passover at the appointed time. However, He did not put up with those who chose to abstain. He even allowed strangers among them to celebrate along with the Israelites. It's clear that God rewarded faith and obedience, even if the person was not an Israelite by birth. He did not tolerate unbelief or disobedience in His own people. For "without faith, it is impossible to please [God]" (Heb. 11:6).

PRESENCE

Read Numbers 9:15-23.

When did the cloud cover the tabernacle?

What was its appearance at night?

This was not the first time the cloud appeared. In Exodus 13, after the people of Israel had celebrated the first Passover, it says, "And the LORD went before them by day in a pillar of cloud to lead them along the way, and by night in a pillar of fire to give them light, that they might travel by day and by night " (v. 21).

How kind of the Lord to give His children exactly what they needed. He made His presence visible and its appearance appropriate for their need. He knew the wilderness could be disorienting, so He made His presence unmistakable.

In what disorienting circumstances have you experienced the kind presence of God?

Exodus and Numbers aren't the only place we find God used cloud imagery to communicate His presence.

Look up the following New Testament texts and record what you find:

LUKE 9:34-36

ACTS 1:9-11

Why do you think God was associated with clouds?

I don't know the definitive answer, but I have some thoughts. Clouds are usually high in the sky, beyond human reach, but here, the Lord brought them low to the earth. The people didn't ascend to where God was; He descended to where they were. And when Christ returns, He will come in the same way: riding upon the clouds again to gather His own.

I want you to underline (or make note of) this phrase at the beginning of Numbers 9:16: "So it was always . . ." Your version may say something like, "It remained that way continuously" (CSB).

The Lord isn't fickle. He doesn't give or remove His presence on a whim. As you'll see in the rest of our study, He doesn't even withdraw His presence when His people complain and rebel against Him. His commitment is to be with us always.

> **Another place in Scripture has a comforting "always." Fill it in below.**
>
> *And behold, I am with you _____, to the end of the age.*
>
> MATTHEW 28:20b

As Christians, we don't have to go looking for His presence. He is always with us. However, we do get to look for how He is working in our midst. I love how Gordon J. Wenham puts it:

> Like the tabernacle, the Christian's body is no empty tent, but a temple for the Spirit (1 Cor. 6:19). Filled by the Spirit he may follow in his Lord's footsteps and resist the temptations of Satan even in the wilderness (Luke 4:1ff). "Let the fiery, cloudy pillar lead me all my journey through."[7]

I have the tendency to think that if only I had a visible cloud by day and a brightly burning pillar by night to remind me of God's presence, I wouldn't struggle with believing God or obeying Him. The truth is, if we are Christians, He is present in us. He is closer than a cloud. We are now His tabernacle, the place of His dwelling. But we, like the Israelites, are prone to forget His very real presence with us, in us. Praise God that His grace is sufficient!

Is the concept that God is with you always hard for you to believe?

Take a moment to write an honest prayer to Him about the truth that He is with you always. It could be as simple as the father's prayer in Mark 9:24: "I believe; help my unbelief!"

PASSAGE

Read Numbers 10:1-10.

The Israelites were so close to taking their first step away from Sinai and toward the promised land. To get such a large amount of people moving at the same time was going to take some serious coordination. Sure, they could see when the cloud or the fire had moved, but to get into the formation prescribed in Numbers 2 and 3, they needed a drum major. (All my marching band nerds are giddy!)

I was in marching band in middle school, and I loved it. We were a military marching band. If you've seen the Fightin' Texas Aggie Band march at a football game, that's what we were like (except less intricate and smaller with cracking voices and braces). The drum major led the band with various blows of her whistle that cued us for what formation came next in the routine. One time, when I was a majorette (that's a mini-drum major who led one line of the many lines of band members), I didn't follow the drum major. My line turned left when all the other lines turned right. It was not a pretty sight. I got the worst chewing out of my life in front of the whole band (a middle-schooler's worst nightmare). It was my fault. The drum major had made it easy: follow her, listen for her cues, and all would be fine. I chose to go my own way, and it turned out not fine.

Moses and Aaron didn't have a whistle. Instead, they had two silver trumpets that communicated to Israel how and when to march through the wilderness. The various blows of the trumpet required different responses.

In what circumstances were they to blow the trumpets (v. 2)?

The Lord had thought through everything. The blasts of the trumpets alerted the people of God's movement, and they responded in obedience to His call.

I am so tempted to push through the rest of chapter 10, but I think now is a good time to pause before the cloud moves, the trumpets sound, and the people finally set out. We'll pick back up in chapter 10 tomorrow, friends. Until then, consider the Lord's deliverance in your life.

How has He provided? How has He made His presence known to you?

His previous faithfulness is always a good indication of His future provision, no matter what the wilderness may hold.

DAY FOUR
TOWARD THE PROMISED LAND

Pause. Breathe. Pray.

After eleven months in the wilderness of Sinai, where they received the Law and God's promises, the Israelites set out for the promised land through the wilderness of Paran. I know it's been a minute, but we get to break out the map for the first time since Session Two!

Turn to page 224 and locate the wilderness of Sinai. Draw a short line from Mount Sinai toward Hazeroth in the Desert of Paran.

Read Numbers 10:11-36.

In verse 12 how did the people of Israel "set out"?

Write the tribes and Levites in the order they set out below.

1. _____   8. _____

2. _____   9. _____

3. _____   10. _____

(Tabernacle was taken down.)   11. _____

4. _____   12. _____

5. _____   13. _____

6. _____   14. _____

7. _____   15. _____

Circle the Kohathites.

What were they carrying?

Why was it important they were placed at this spot in the procession (v. 21)?

This was no small caravan. This was an entire nation on the move. Think about how long it must have taken for each tribe to travel to the spot where the cloud landed if the tabernacle was already set up when the Kohathites got there! The tent of meeting was large with layers of coverings and specific instructions for how to put everything in its proper place. It must have taken an extensive amount of time to put together again. It appears they had plenty!

> **Look back at the drawing on page 27 and notice where each tribe was encamped. Compare the tribes' placement with the order in which they struck out.**
>
> **Write the order in which they marched according to the cardinal direction (north, south, east, west) when camped. I'll get you started.**
>
> **East: Judah, Issachar, Zebulun, then . . .**

What practical implications did this have on striking out from and setting up camp?

The Israelites traveled through the wilderness in a military formation. They were not on vacation. This was not a road trip to see the sights. God was preparing His people to enter the promised land like they meant it. He did not lead them this far only to leave them to haphazardly navigate the wilderness. God had a plan and provision to get His children all the way there.

While we might not be traversing the Sinai Peninsula with our whole families in tow, we can still experience the wilderness metaphorically. The wilderness might be any circumstance in which we find ourselves that is unfamiliar, distressing, lonely, and marked by intense longing. Maybe it's the waiting and longing for a child, a job, a ministry, or a spouse. Maybe your relationship with the Lord has felt labored, diluted, or dry. Or maybe you're in a new situation, town, church, or position, and you're trying to find your "new normal."

If you are in a wilderness season, does it feel haphazard? Do you feel aimless? Flesh that out here. Be willing to pour out the contents of your heart and realize that the Lord already knows what's in it.

HELP

In Numbers 10:29-32 Moses had a conversation with his brother-in-law, Hobab. What's the gist of it?

Are you surprised by any of it? If so, what part?

Here are my questions:

- Was the cloud by day and fire by night not enough?

- Couldn't they just stop in the exact place the cloud/fire stopped?

- Why would they need Hobab's help?

- Isn't God's general direction sufficient?

Scripture doesn't record Moses being rebuked by God for asking Hobab to serve as their "eyes" (v. 31). According to what we have in Scripture, the Lord didn't say, *If only you hadn't trusted Hobab more than you trusted Me.* So I think we can safely assume that Moses' request for Hobab to continue on with them was not a lack of faith in God's guidance. Moses knew the Lord would lead them on the first stage of their journey, but he also knew that water and food were hard to come by in the desert. Hobab was a Midianite—a people well acquainted with life in the wilderness. Hobab likely knew what it took to survive in the desolate environment. It seems that Moses wasn't lacking faith; he was being wise.

While this interaction doesn't take up too much space in the overall story of Israel's journey, I found my attention drawn to it. I think many of us can make an error one of two ways. Either we rely on the Lord alone without seeking counsel, or we find so many counselors that we miss the Lord's guidance. I tend toward the former. It looks "holy" and "righteous," but I think in my pride, I don't want to have to ask for help.

> **Look up Proverbs 11:14. What does it say about seeking counsel or guidance?**

> **How about you? Which do you tend toward—seeking no counsel or seeking too much? Why?**

ONWARD!

> **Read Numbers 10:29-36.**

The time had come. Israel was finally on her way to the promised land! We can almost hear the excitement in Moses' voice as we read these verses. He was full of faith and firmly confident in God's guidance and provision.

> **When Moses entreated Hobab to go with them, he said God promised something to Israel (v. 29). What did he say?**

> **How far did they make it in the first stage of travel (v. 33)?**

What went before them (v. 33)?

What did Moses say as the ark set out (v. 35)?

What did Moses say when the ark rested (v. 36)?

The two sayings that are quoted in verses 35 and 36 are referred to as "The Song of the Ark."[8] David riffed on the second part in Psalm 68.

Circle the phrases in the Psalm that correlate with Moses' words.

God shall arise, his enemies shall be scattered;

and those who hate him shall flee before him!

As smoke is driven away, so you shall drive them away;

as wax melts before fire,

so the wicked shall perish before God!

But the righteous shall be glad;

they shall exult before God;

They shall be jubilant with joy!

PSALM 68:1-3

Imagine the enthusiasm of that day! Hear the frenzied chatter, the children buzzing with expectation, their parents herding and hushing them with some difficulty because they, too, could hardly contain their excitement. There's so much hope, so much anticipation!

Can you identify with this? Have you ever set out on a vacation, a new adventure, a new quest, pregnant with aspiration? You made the plans. You packed all the things. What could possibly go wrong?

Maybe some of you could identify with another group—the ones who believe God will come through—but you're a little anxious about how this will all work out. You're excited but soberly.

Which resonates with you?

There's good news (as always with God) for the expectant and the anxious who trust the Lord. He promises to do good to His people. As we follow Israel from Mount Sinai into the wilderness of Paran, I can't help but think of Psalm 139.

Turn to Psalm 139:1-6 and read aloud (if possible).

The Israelites didn't know what lay before them. They didn't know their faith would be tested and found lacking. They didn't know the journey would take much longer than they expected. But God knew. And He still kept His presence with them. He did not forsake His people. He hemmed them in. He kept His hand upon them.

I don't know where you are with the Lord. I don't know if you're in the midst of the wilderness or on the cusp of the promised land. But He knows.

Take a few minutes to write out your thoughts or a prayer as a response to Psalm 139:1-6.

DAY FIVE
SPEED BUMPS

Pause. Breathe. Pray.

Before we look at the text for today's personal study, glance back at Numbers 10:29-36. What's the overall tone?

Now look at Numbers 11:1. What shift in tone do you see?

As a mother of three children (one tween and two teens), I can completely identify with this scenario. Too many times I have started on a trip or endeavor with our family, bright-eyed, bushy-tailed, and ready for adventure, and I have been met with the moans and cries of my children. "How much longer? I'm so bored! Why couldn't I have stayed with my friends?"

Things for Moses weren't that different. He couldn't wait to get moving toward the promised land. His hope was firmly in the Lord being good to His people. Sure, he knew it wouldn't be easy, but he also knew they were free, and the Lord was with them!

And the people complained . . . (Num. 11:1).

Awesome. All of that work to set out toward the promised land, the miracles God had performed in front of their eyes, and the first words out of their mouths was a complaint?

Refer to Numbers 11:1-3 to answer the following:

How did God know they were complaining? Did they come to Him about their concerns?

At what point did the people cry out to someone? To whom did they cry out?

I know none of you have probably ever complained to people who can do absolutely nothing to solve your problems. I certainly haven't. (I hope you can hear the sarcasm dripping from that statement.) The Israelites weren't really looking for an answer to their complaints. They complained to complain.

Listen, I know they had plenty of reasons to be uncomfortable. Full disclosure: I have only "camped" once and vowed never to do it again unless a soft bed and a clean bathroom are nearby. I can only imagine the conditions the Israelites had to endure. Still, they had the ear and the presence of the one true God in their midst. He could certainly do something about their discomfort; He could strengthen their faith and endurance or provide for their needs. All they had to do was ask.

How did the Lord respond to their complaints?

What parts of the camp were burned?

What did they name the place where this happened? What does the name mean?

We will come back to this idea of words and fire as we wrap up today's personal study. For now, let's keep moving.

Let's hop back to Exodus for a moment.

Read Exodus 12:38. According to this verse, who went with the Israelites toward the promised land?

Numbers 11:4 calls this group of people "the rabble." *Rabble* is derived from a verb meaning *to collect*.[9] "These are a collection of people who have attached themselves to the Israelites."[10] In this case, the *rabble* is a group of non-Israelites who have joined the caravan toward the promised land.

Read Numbers 11:4-15.

What specific complaint did "the rabble" make?

What did they miss about Egypt (v. 5)?

Read Exodus 3:7-9. Why were the Israelites in the wilderness instead of Egypt?

What's problematic about their memory?

Read Exodus 16:31 and Numbers 11:7-9. What had God provided for them to eat?

Manna was the miraculous bread from heaven that required nothing of them to produce. All they had to do was gather enough of it in the morning to last for the day. The same thing happened every day. The only variation was for the Sabbath. They were to gather enough for two days so they wouldn't have to gather it on the Sabbath. The Lord preserved its freshness for them. How kind of Him!

It seemed their taste buds had reached their manna limit. Under the surface, though, we see that it's more than the lack of variety. They were longing for Egypt or their skewed memory of it.

I have a terrible habit of dreaming up the perfect home—the floor plan, the style, the landscaping, the acreage. Unfortunately, it's never the home we're living in at the moment. When we moved from our last home to the current one, I couldn't wait to ditch the one-story, seventies ranch-style home for the cute, two-story farmhouse with the trees. After living in the farmhouse for a few years with living quarters stacked on top of each other, I can reminisce about the ranch home's spaciousness—when I had to walk all through the house calling for my children like a game of Marco Polo.

Has the Lord ever provided something for you that was right and good but lost the luster it had at first? Maybe it's your marriage, your home, or a job you once prayed for but now resent. Write about whatever comes to mind below.

Are you tempted to think longingly back to another situation or provision that He called you out of and freed you from? Expound on that here.

What was Moses' emotional response to the people's complaining (Num. 11:10)?

To whom did he go with his complaints (v. 11)?

Record Moses' exact words below (vv. 11-15).

I praise God for bits of Scripture like this one which reveal Moses' complaint to God. It makes me feel a little less crazy. Moses went for it. He didn't hold back before the Lord. At first I thought he was being a little dramatic, but then I put myself in his shoes. He was responsible for a lot of people. They were hungry. They were tired. They were ready to just be somewhere, anywhere but in the middle of the wilderness. The difference between Moses' complaint and Israel's is that he took it to the Lord. He didn't murmur to Aaron or Miriam. He poured out his heart to God—the only One who could do anything to truly help him.

Is there something that has burdened you today that you haven't taken to the Lord yet?

Have you taken it to someone else who can't really do anything about it?

Read Psalm 121:1-2. Where does our help come from?

Write out a prayer here to the Lord, telling Him what burdens you are carrying and asking forgiveness for not coming to Him in the first place.

Let me say this: Nothing is wrong with confessing to a friend the burden you are carrying or the longing that isn't being fulfilled the way you'd hoped. Just don't stop (or start) there. It can feel like a load off to share with another person, but the Lord wants the opportunity to come through for you. Take Him up on it!

What invitation does the Lord give us in Matthew 11:28?

ELDERS APPOINTED

While the Lord responded to overhearing the people's complaints with fire, He listened to Moses' complaint and gave a solution.

According to Numbers 11:16-17, what did the Lord tell Moses to do?

God didn't snap His fingers and make it easy. He gave Moses more work to do, but it was work that led to rest and fellowship. We see in verses 24-25 that God did exactly what He said He would do when Moses obeyed and gathered the seventy elders. He came down and spoke to Moses and then took some of the Spirit and put it on them.

Why seventy elders? John D. Currid explains that "The number 'seventy' is often used of such a group of elders (see Exod. 24:9), and it is a symbolic number that reflects totality and completeness."[11]

How did the Spirit manifest on the seventy elders? For how long?

Refer to Numbers 11:26-30 to answer the next questions.

Who was Joshua?

What "problem" did a young man bring to Moses' attention? How did Joshua react (v. 28)?

How did Moses respond to Joshua's reaction (v. 29)?

Oh, Joshua, I have been there. Young in my leadership experience, I have scoffed at others not doing it "the right way." Oof. I have missed the heart of someone or some ministry because they didn't follow the rules I had made for them.

We don't know exactly what this "prophesying" looked like, but it was noticeable enough that the young man in the camp recognized it in Eldad and Medad. Little did Moses know that his desire for all God's people to be prophets and have the Spirit on them was exactly a part of God's plan.

In Acts 2 the disciples and followers of Christ gathered together to celebrate Pentecost. All of a sudden, the sound of a mighty rushing wind blew through the room where they were gathered and divided into tongues of fire that rested on each person there. "And they were all filled with the Holy Spirit" (v. 4a).

Moses' desire came true then and continues to come true every time someone puts his or her faith in Christ. When we receive Christ, we are given a new heart, and He puts His Spirit in us. (See Ezek. 36:27.) Thus, we should have something noticeably different about us—the mark of His Spirit.

> **What evidence do you see of the Spirit in your own life? In the lives of others?**

> **Do people sometimes react like the young man in Numbers 11 when people walk in the Spirit? What might that look like?**

THE MEAT SWEATS

There's a phenomenon that hasn't been scientifically substantiated but, if you've ever eaten too much meat at one time, you know it exists. It's called the "meat sweats," and Israel was about to experience something much worse.

> **Read Numbers 11:31-35.**

God equated Israel's complaining with rejecting Him. They didn't want Him; they wanted Egypt—a cheap substitute.

> **What truth about human nature did Jesus teach us in Luke 6:45?**

The Israelites didn't just have a mouth problem. They had a heart problem. They didn't believe (nor did they want) God to come through for them. God answered the people's complaint by giving them exactly what they said they wanted: meat.

What was the result (Num. 11:33)?

What did they name the place where these events occurred? What does the name mean (v. 34)?

I sat in our recovery ministry gathering not long ago among many people who had been, like Israel, choosing Egypt over the Lord. I have been one of them, and I still have the propensity to choose an idol over God. The teacher who spoke that night touched on this very scenario. He said that worship isn't a matter of *if* but of *what*. We worship something or someone. Will it be the Lord, some thing, or someone else? He pointed out that most often, God won't flex His muscles to show us how much better He is than the substitute we worship. Instead, He will let us chase that idol. He will give us what we want.

Describe a time when the Lord let you have something you had been craving as an idol. What was the ultimate result?

ET TU, MIRIAM AND AARON?

As if the people's grumbling, Joshua's naivete, and a plague weren't enough, Moses faced opposition in his own tent.

Summarize Miriam and Aaron's complaint found in Numbers 12:1-2.

Miriam and Aaron looked for even the smallest thing to discredit Moses. They were jealous of what seemed to be the exclusivity of his leadership (even though the Lord put His Spirit on the seventy elders!). They thought, *Why not us? We could do just as well, if not better!* The Lord overheard them and called all three to the principal's office, so to speak. He rebuked them, saying (my translation), *Moses is my man, so much so that I don't speak to him in dreams, visions, and riddles, but face-to-face. Why weren't you afraid of speaking against him?*

Read what happened next in Numbers 12:10-16.

The anger of the Lord was kindled against them. Miriam paid the price. She became leprous. Moses begged God to heal Miriam (proving that he indeed was the meekest person on earth).

What did Miriam and Aaron's complaining reveal about their hearts?

Why do you think the Lord didn't listen to Moses but allowed Miriam to suffer for seven days?

PLAYING WITH FIRE

Themes are weaving in and out of our reading today: words and fire.

Fill the table below with each instance of the words and a corresponding fire/kindling.

WORDS	FIRE/KINDLING

The Book of James tells the truth about the human tongue: it's small but can set an entire forest on fire (figuratively speaking). (See Jas. 3:5.) God's burning response to Israel's complaining was fitting. As the fire consumed the outlying areas of the camp and as His anger was "kindled" (v. 9) against the rabble and Miriam and Aaron, so our untamed tongues bring destruction to others and ourselves.

Read James 3:5-6.

Have you felt the burn of another's words or as a result of your own?

Words can do tremendous damage. There is hope for us, though. The fire of the Lord doesn't just consume; it refines and purifies. If we have complained to complain, gossiped, boasted, or put others down and have confessed and humbly repented, He is faithful and just to forgive us our sins and cleanse (purify!) us from all unrighteousness (1 John 1:9). The same tongue that destroyed can be used to confess and bless.

We get another chance. Thank You, Jesus.

If this resonated with you, take a minute to write down your thoughts or confession.

Y'all made it through Session Three! We are well on our way into the wilderness alongside Israel, but we still have much further to go. However, we don't go alone. He is with us.

I've provided some discussion questions here to get the conversation started. Feel free to discuss what you learned throughout the week of study, ask any questions you may have, and share what God is teaching you.

DISCUSSION QUESTIONS

The people around us can lead us to godly cooperation and care or foster discouragement and murmuring. Take some time to describe and honor those in your community who consistently point you toward holy living—what about them helps keep you encouraged? How does it challenge you to see their example?

Living in community means that our strengths and weaknesses are exposed. In your own heart and your own community, do you struggle to let others see the messy parts of your life? Explain why it's difficult sometimes. Describe a time you've been blessed by "being known" in your community.

Read John 17:20-23 aloud in your group. With this passage in mind, what might godly community look like—in theory? Practically?

Teaching sessions available for purchase or rent at *LifeWay.com/WithUsInTheWilderness*

DISTRUST, DETOUR, AND DISCONTENT

So the LORD said to Aaron, "You and your sons and your father's house with you shall bear iniquity connected with the sanctuary, and you and your sons with you shall bear iniquity connected with your priesthood."

NUMBERS 18:1

I SPY THE PROMISED LAND

Pause. Breathe. Pray.

Last week ended on a rough note for Moses. As we will discover together this week, the division Moses experienced with his siblings was just the beginning. A lot is going on in chapter 13, so we will hop right in with a geographical activity!

The last time we pulled out the map, we traced Israel's short route (three days journey) from Mount Sinai. At the end of chapter 12, we see that the Israelites set out from Hazeroth and camped in the wilderness of Paran.

1. **On page 224, draw a line (with a little bit of movement) from Hazeroth to the Red Sea.**

2. **Follow the coastline of the Red Sea with your pen/pencil for a bit and then land in Kadesh Barnea. According to the *ESV Study Bible*, "Kadesh is a large oasis about 50 miles (80 km) southwest of Beersheba."[1]**

    Read Numbers 13:1-24.

    What did God tell Moses to do?

    In God's instructions to Moses (v. 2), what did He say about the land of Canaan?

The verses on the next page are all promises God made to Moses and to the people of Israel. Even if the people didn't hear it directly from God's mouth, they heard it through His chosen mouthpiece—Moses.

In each of the following passages:
1. Underline God's promise regarding the land.
2. Circle the words "I am the LORD your God" each time they appear.

*I will bring you into the land that I swore to give
to Abraham, to Isaac, and to Jacob. I will give
it to you for a possession. I am the LORD.*

EXODUS 6:8

*But I have said to you, "You shall inherit their land, and I will give
it to you to possess, a land flowing with milk and honey." I am
the LORD your God, who has separated you from the peoples.*

LEVITICUS 20:24

*I am the LORD your God, who brought you out of the land of
Egypt to give you the land of Canaan, and to be your God.*

LEVITICUS 25:38

Remember, the Lord promised the land of Canaan to Abraham and his
descendants. He reminded His people of this promise over and over again. It
was the very reason they found themselves out of Egypt and in the midst of
the wilderness.

In each verse above, God reminded the Israelites who He is. Why do
you think He did that?

The Lord always keeps His promises. He delivered the Israelites by signs
and wonders from Egypt, just like He promised (Ex. 6:1). God sustained His
children in the wilderness, just like He promised (Ex. 16). God's very presence
was among them, just like He promised (Ex. 33:14). If God promises He will
do something, nothing can stop Him.

How does God's track record of promises keep encouraging you today?

Let's circle back to Numbers 13 and look at the men whom Moses chose. List them in order along with their tribe (vv. 3-16).

SPY	TRIBE	SPY	TRIBE
1.		7.	
2.		8.	
3.		9.	
4.		10.	
5.		11.	
6.		12.	

Draw a star by Caleb and Hoshea. (This will be important later.)

In verse 16 what did Moses call Hoshea?

Write down what you already know about Caleb and Joshua.

Place yourself in the spies' shoes. You've just been drafted to go into a foreign land and spy on the unknown enemies who live there. What would you be thinking? Feeling?

Since God had already promised to give Israel the land, why do you think He instructed Moses to send in spies?

At first blush, it looks like the spies' mission was tactical. They were sent to see what the land was like, assess the people living in it, and determine the strength of their fortifications. But it also could have been an opportunity to build the people's faith. Their trip to Canaan could have been a faith-filled exploration of the good land God had promised.

Let's turn to the map on page 224 and with another colored pen or pencil, trace the route of the spies.

Start at Kadesh Barnea then go:

- north through Negeb;
- between Beersheba and Hormah;
- through Hebron;
- just east of Shechem;
- through Beth Shean;
- just west of Hazor;
- stop just south of Lebo-Hamath.
- Draw an arrow at the end of your line.

THE REPORT OF THE SPIES

Read Numbers 13:25-33.

How long were the spies in Canaan (v. 25)?

The trip from Kadesh Barnea to Lebo-Hamath is approximately two hundred fifty miles.[2] Forty days would have been a reasonable amount of time for the spies to travel through the area and accomplish the tasks they were given. If you've spent some time studying the Scriptures, your attention might have piqued at the occurrence of forty days.

- The Lord sent rain upon the earth in the great flood for forty days and forty nights (Gen. 7:12).

- For forty days, Goliath came out against Saul's army, defying and provoking them, until David showed up and killed him with a stone from his slingshot (1 Sam. 17:16).

- Jesus fasted forty days and forty nights while in the wilderness before being tempted by Satan (Matt. 4:2).

Do you see a common theme among the instances above, including the spies' journey?

Most often in Scripture, forty days is associated with a time of testing. The Lord tested Noah's endurance in the flood; the spies tested the quality of the land; Goliath tested Israel's faith in the Lord to deliver her enemies into her hands; Satan tested Jesus, who proved faithful, in the wilderness before His public earthly ministry.

While the Lord does not tempt us (Jas. 1:13), He certainly allows us to be tested. In Luke 22:31-32, we see Jesus telling Peter that Satan had asked to sift Peter like wheat. The Book of James tells us, "Count it all joy, my brothers, when you meet trials of various kinds, for you know that the *testing of your faith* produces steadfastness" (1:2-3, *emphasis mine*). Testing isn't a bad thing, but it isn't an easy thing either.

Do you feel like you are in the midst of a testing season? If so, what does it look like for you?

If you are tired from the testing, may I encourage you, friend? Jesus knows. He knows what you're going through. He knows because He has been there. It might not be the exact same circumstances, but He is not unaware or lacking empathy. Go to Him. Just as Jesus prayed for Peter (Luke 22:32), the Spirit will intercede for you (Rom. 8:26).

Let's look at the spies' checklist recorded in Numbers 13:17-20. Did they cover them all? Place a checkmark by each task they obediently completed.

_____ Assess the land.

_____ Assess the people.

_____ Assess the cities (fortified or not).

_____ Bring back fruit.

Beside each item above, provide details of what they found according to verses 25-29.

The spies told Moses and Aaron that the land was all God promised it would be, but with one caveat—the people living there. I can almost hear the spies now, *We've got some good news and some bad news. Which would you like to hear first?*

Who spoke up after the spies gave their initial report (v. 30)?

Did he contradict the facts of the report?

Record his exact words.

Caleb was unfazed by what he saw in Canaan because he knew the Lord had promised to give the land to them. In his mind, it was already theirs! He had faith in God's ability to come through for them no matter what.

How did the spies' story change after Caleb's effort to rally the people to faith and obedience (vv. 32-33)?

The problem with the spies' "bad report" (v. 32) was that they compared the strength of the people in Canaan with their own strength. It wasn't by their strength they were taken out of Egypt. It wasn't by their strength the Red Sea parted before them. It wasn't by their strength they produced manna or quail.

What made them think it was their strength that would require them to take the promised land?

The people of God can still struggle with sliding back into self-reliance. In Galatians 3 Paul rebuked the church for operating in her own strength (the flesh) instead of continuing in the Spirit. He reminded them it is by faith in what Christ has purchased for us on the cross that we continue to be perfected by Him. It is not achieved by trying harder and keeping all the rules.

The promised land can represent all sorts of things in the believer's life. Most importantly, it symbolizes eternal life in Christ. By our strength, we can't measure up. We can't get there. We fall miserably short of God's standard of holiness. But by believing in Christ we get there. We get Him. Not only does Jesus cover our sin and imperfections with His blood and perfect life, He gives us the Holy Spirit who works in and through us to make us more like Him.

Maybe the promised land for you (in addition to eternal life in Christ) is freedom from a habit, sin, or thought pattern that refuses to die. You are desperate to be free, but it seems like it's impossible. With you, it is. With God, it's not.

What's your "promised land"? In other words, what are some promises you see in Scripture for your life that don't seem to be coming true or that seem downright impossible?

Here's what I've experienced in my thirty years of walking with Jesus: The Lord loves using the small, weak, and insignificant to humble the large, strong, and self-important.

Close today with a simple prayer.

Lord, I believe. Help my unbelief. Help me remember that Your grace is sufficient for me and that Your power is made perfect in weakness. With You God, all things are possible. Amen.

REBELLION AND JUDGMENT

Pause. Breathe. Pray.

Have you ever seen a film that had you yelling at the screen as if the characters could hear you? Especially when it's the moment in the movie when you know they are going to make a decision they will regret forever and all you want to do is grab them through the screen and shake them? Or is that just me?

Reading Numbers 14 evokes those same feelings in me. All I want to do is reach through the pages and shake the people of Israel and say, "Don't do it!"

Honestly, there are moments in my past I wish I could reinsert my slightly-more-sanctified self and shout a wake-up call!

How about you? Do you have a moment (or two) you wish you could do the same?

THE PEOPLE REBEL

Read Numbers 14:1-12.

Why were the people raising a loud cry, weeping, and grumbling (vv. 2-3)?

What did they say they wish had happened to them (v. 2)?

What did they say to one another (v. 4)?

Despite all the miracles and wonders they had seen, the people of Israel couldn't believe the Lord would deliver on His promise. In their minds, it was going to be too much for God to handle. He had made a mistake. To Israel, Egypt began to look better and better. (There's that revisionist history again.)

I can remember standing on the edge of freedom from an idol in my life and thinking, *Lord, how can I navigate this? It feels like death. Although my old way of life isn't working, at least it's predictable. At least I know what I'm facing.*

I had never known life without comparing it to someone else's. I didn't know how to be comfortable in the skin and calling God had given only to me. I wanted someone else's story. I wanted to order my life like an item in a catalog: clear skin, outstanding voice, excellent songwriter, notoriety, cozy home with a loving husband and obedient kids, no struggles, no pain, just ease . . . all for only $49.95! Basically, I wanted to be my own god. I wanted what I wanted, when I wanted it, and how I wanted it. But I knew there could only be one God in my life, and I'm not Him. I knew I could find the freedom and satisfaction my heart was longing for in Him, but it was frightening to give up the semblance of control. Ironically (and so like Him), He gave me the things I wanted but wrapped in different packaging. And the things He didn't give me (and there's a long list)—I can truly say He is better than all of them.

Have you been there? If so, flesh that out a bit here.

Not only did the people reject God and His plan, they rejected His man, Moses. There's something to be said that they didn't even ask Moses to lead them back. They knew he wasn't going anywhere. Although he had bouts with feeling overwhelmed leading the people, he was unwaveringly faithful to the Lord. The people could have taken their cues from Moses (and Caleb!) and trusted the Lord would deliver Canaan into their hands, but they didn't. Instead of adjusting to the Lord's plan, they adjusted their plan to meet their perceived needs.

In 2 Timothy 4:3-4 Paul warned Timothy—his "son in the faith" (1 Tim. 1:2, CSB) and a pastor—the following:

> *For the time is coming when people will not endure sound teaching, but having itching ears they will accumulate for themselves teachers to suit their own passions, and will turn away from listening to the truth and wander off into myths.*

In the verse on the previous page, underline *turn away* and *wander*.

Over thousands of years, people haven't really changed. Our clothing, hairstyles, and technology may look very different, but our propensity to go our own way hasn't. This is rebellion. It's not always over-the-top. It can be the subtle act of saying, *God, thanks, but no thanks* (turning away) and going our own way (wandering).

The people of God didn't like what they heard, so they looked for a leader who would tickle their ears with the promise of a return to Egypt. They came up to the edge of God's promise and said, *no thanks*, turned away, and, as we will see in the next chapters, wandered for a very long time.

Before Israel headed back, Moses, Aaron, Caleb, and Joshua tried their best to convince them otherwise.

Record and compare the actions of Moses and Aaron, Caleb and Joshua, and the Israelites in Numbers 14. In each column, record what each individual's or group's actions revealed about their hearts.

	HOW THEY REACTED	WHAT THEIR ACTIONS REVEALED ABOUT THEIR HEARTS
Moses and Aaron (v. 5)		
Caleb and Joshua (vv. 6-9)		
The people of Israel (v. 10)		

What stopped the Israelites from carrying out their plan? (Talk about the ultimate mic drop. You can't really argue with the glory of the Lord showing up.)

What did the Lord say He would do in response to Israel's unbelief (v. 12)?

What do God's words recorded in verse 11 reveal about His heart?

MOSES INTERCEDED FOR THE PEOPLE

Read Numbers 14:13-38.

How did Moses respond to the Lord's proposal to start over with him? Make an outline of Moses' appeal to God.

How did Moses appeal to God's character (v. 18)? Do Moses' statements reveal he was more concerned about the Lord's reputation or the well-being of the people?

Have you ever made an appeal to God like this? How have you grounded your request in God's character or promises?

Did the Lord listen to Moses? What was the caveat (vv. 20-24)?

Who escaped God's judgment and why (vv. 24,30)?

What happened to the spies who gave the bad report (vv. 36-37)?

The Lord is perfectly merciful and perfectly just. Our human minds struggle to hold this tension. We see here, though, how it works out. He pardoned the people's sin and judged them accordingly. He gave them what they said they wanted: to die in the wilderness (v. 2). For every day the spies explored the land, He gave them a year wandering in the wilderness. The only thing the people got wrong about their destiny to die in the desert was that their children would become prey. The Lord showed His unmatched mercy by promising the children would know the land their parents rejected.

IN THEIR OWN STRENGTH

Read Numbers 14:39-45.

How did Israel react to God's judgment?

According to Moses, why was this a bad idea?

What was the result of their decision?

Although Israel's direction changed, the Israelites' hearts had not. They were still set on doing things their way and in their own strength. In 2 Corinthians 7 the apostle Paul made a distinction between worldly grief (that we see here in the people of Israel) and godly grief.

As it is, I rejoice, not because you were grieved, but because you were grieved into repenting. For you felt a godly grief, so that you suffered no loss through us. For godly grief produces a repentance that leads to salvation without regret, whereas worldly grief produces death.

Underline what godly grief produces.

Circle what worldly grief produces.

How did Israel exhibit worldly grief?

What could it have looked like for the Israelites to display godly grief?

Look up the following examples of godly grief from Scripture. What are some common responses to godly grief?

ESTHER 4:3

JONAH 3:6-9

As a kid, worldly grief often looked like being sad that I got caught breaking a rule or that I had to suffer consequences rather than being truly broken over my sin. This hasn't changed much as an adult either. I can find myself more frustrated, grieved, or ashamed that I was called out for my sin than over the sin itself.

102   WITH US IN THE WILDERNESS

Are there any areas of your life where you have experienced worldly grief at the expense of godly grief and repentance? Take this moment to ask God to give you the grace to be more broken over your sin than sad that you are paying the cost of getting caught.

This was a devastating chapter. All this time we have watched the Lord prepare the Israelites to take hold of the land God had promised to them, and the Israelites fell short. They were so close! While the people may have departed for the promised land without the ark of the covenant of the LORD or Moses (Num. 14:44), the Lord never took His presence from the camp. He didn't pull up the pegs of the tabernacle. He didn't remove the cloud or snuff out the pillar of fire. He stuck with them. Not only that, He offered hope to the next generation.

I don't know where you are, but I know that the Lord doesn't give up on His own. He went so far as to send His own Son to be faithful when He knew we could not. Nothing can keep us from that kind of love. Close today meditating on Romans 8:31-39.

> *What then shall we say to these things? If God is for us, who can be against us? He who did not spare his own Son but gave him up for us all, how will he not also with him graciously give us all things? Who shall bring any charge against God's elect? It is God who justifies. Who is to condemn? Christ Jesus is the one who died—more than that, who was raised—who is at the right hand of God, who indeed is interceding for us. Who shall separate us from the love of Christ? Shall tribulation, or distress, or persecution, or famine, or nakedness, or danger, or sword? As it is written,*
>
> *"For your sake we are being killed all the day long; we are regarded as sheep to be slaughtered."*
>
> *No, in all these things we are more than conquerors through him who loved us. For I am sure that neither death nor life, nor angels nor rulers, nor things present nor things to come, nor powers, nor height nor depth, nor anything else in all creation, will be able to separate us from the love of God in Christ Jesus our Lord.*
>
> ROMANS 8:31-39

DAY THREE
LOOK, REMEMBER, DO

Pause. Breathe. Pray.

We have two teenagers in our home right now, and, while it has stretched our parenting muscles to new lengths, we have thoroughly enjoyed seeing them come into their own. As their mother, I want so badly to protect them from anything that might cause them pain or hardship. Fortunately, I can put rules and boundaries in place, but, unfortunately, I cannot make them abide by them. (I also can't encase them in bubble wrap and forbid them to leave the house either. Go figure.) What has surprised us the most about parenting teenagers is that they can be much harsher on themselves than we would ever be toward them. Sure, we have consequences for poor choices and appropriate punishment for disobedience, but our goal isn't to decimate their lives. If anything, we want their flourishing above all.

I wonder what the Israelites thought of the Lord's "parenting." I wonder if they were surprised by His promise to their children. Were they incredulous? Grateful? Relieved?

On the surface, Numbers 15 seems like just another bunch of rules. As we read between the lines, though, I hope you'll see God's mercy and faithfulness woven throughout.

Read Numbers 15:1-21.

Did the Lord say "If you come into the land" or "When you come into the land" (v. 2)? What does that imply?

For whom were these laws given?

Whom does the Lord include with the children of Israel in observing these laws (v. 14)?

List the types of food that are to be sacrificed.

What phrase is repeated in verses 3,7,10,13, and 14?

What aromas do you find especially pleasing?

Speaking of "pleasing," what does it reveal about God that the offerings outlined in the chapter were a "pleasing aroma to the Lord"?

The commentators of the *ESV Study Bible's* notes on Numbers 15 made this wonderful observation: "The imagery of sacrifice is drawn from that of a meal: the worshiper must act as the generous host and give to God all that he would give an important guest (Gen. 18:1-8)."[3]

The Lord is not a grumpy old man who's hard to please and just waits for us to do something wrong. He is the God who delights in pleasing aromas and the proximity of His people. Remember, all these rules and laws about sacrifices and offerings are to bring God's people closer to Him.

Not only is God confident that He will bring His people into the promised land, He is confident in its abundance. All the measures for the grain, wheat, wine, and meat are considerable. The only way the people could fulfill the requirements was if the land was abundantly productive.

UNINTENTIONAL AND INTENTIONAL SINS

Read Numbers 15:22-36.

What's the difference between the unintentional sin committed in verses 22-26 and that in verses 27-29? (Hint: who committed the sin?)

How is the person's sin in verse 30 described? What do you think this means?

To act with a "high hand" is to act from a place of pride. Some translations say "defiantly" or "presumptuously." The word originally used here can also be translated *lofty*.[4] In this case, it conveys a willful disobedience of God's law.

What's the difference between God's response to unintentional sin and the sin committed in verses 30-31?

How do the preceding verses help you understand what is described in verses 32-36?

Intention matters to God. You can't trick Him. He is not fooled by lip service. He sees the heart. He knows whether we sin unintentionally or defiantly. Sin has consequences whether we are aware of what we're doing or not. It affects our relationship with God and others.

When we sin unintentionally and become aware of it, we don't have to offer sacrifices anymore. We get to embrace the forgiveness afforded to us by the cross of Christ—the ultimate sacrifice. We don't have to sit in shame or beat ourselves up over our mistakes. They're covered.

When we sin intentionally, when we say, *God, I know what You require of me, but I don't want to obey You*, we still have hope. The Lord extends His offer of grace through confession and repentance. I never grow tired of hearing 1 John 1:9: "If we confess our sins, he is faithful and just to forgive us our sins and to cleanse us from all unrighteousness."

But be sober-minded about this and don't presume upon God's grace. Rather, take to heart the words Jesus spoke to the woman caught in adultery after Jesus did not condemn her and her accusers could not either: "Go and sin no more" (John 8:11b, NLT).

As you read about intentional and unintentional sin, does anything come to mind? Maybe an offense someone brought to you? Or a sin you continue to justify instead of coming clean and pulling it into the open?

If there's something you want to bring into the light, take it to the Lord first and then share it with someone you trust.

LOOK, REMEMBER, AND DO

Read Numbers 15:37-41.

What were the people instructed to put on the corners of their garments (v. 38)?

What was the purpose of the tassels (vv. 39-40)?

After the Lord gave instructions for sinning unintentionally and intentionally, He gave a better option: look, remember, and do. He knew His people needed help remembering. We too easily forget His goodness—that His law is for our good—that flourishing is found when we submit to Him. Because He knew His people's tendency to forget and go their own way, He told them to make tassels of remembrance.

Blue is a color associated with royalty (Esth. 8:15) and divinity. (Remember, the ark of the covenant was wrapped in a blue cloth; the curtains in the tabernacle were blue; the high priests had blue on their garments). So when the Israelite looked at the blue thread hanging from the corners of his garment, he was reminded "that he belonged to 'a kingdom of priests and a holy nation' (Exod. 19:6)."[5]

All sorts of needless pain results from spiritual amnesia, especially when we forget who and whose we are: the beloved children of God. I heard a pastor preach on this topic recently. He referenced a study done on the effectiveness of different treatments for addiction, cigarette smoking in particular. The researchers found that those who did not primarily identify themselves as smokers found it easier to quit smoking than those who did. For example, the person who said, "I am a person who smokes occasionally" had a better rate of success quitting than the person who said, "I'm a smoker."[6] *Their behavior flowed out of their identity.*

The Lord made us this way. He knew our best chance at obedience was to remember we are His. He gave tassels to His people as they entered the promised land so they would look at them, remember they are the children of the Lord their God who brought them out of Egypt, and do what the Lord told them to do.

Do you struggle to remember you are a beloved child of God? Is there something you could do (a physical reminder, like the tassels) to help you remember?

Read Luke 8:43-48.

Who touched Jesus?

What did she want healing for?

According to Numbers 5:1-4, where would she have been if she had lived among Israel in the wilderness? For how long?

What did she touch?

How did Jesus respond to her?

Here was a woman on the fringes who had no hope left but to grab the fringes of the Healer's garment. She wasn't "worthy" of the garment, but she held onto the physical reminder to God's people that they are His. Jesus, in turn, called her Daughter. He affirmed her faith in the Lord and her place in His kingdom.

Nowhere else is healing and wholeness found but in Jesus. Because I know God is all-knowing, I imagine He had that woman in view when He saw His people gathering the threads together and sewing them onto their clothes. God the Father knew that God the Son would wear that garment Himself, fulfilling all the Law, healing the sick, the blind, and lame, and redeeming His people.[7] The Lord required much but supplied much through Jesus. Praise be to Him!

How has the Lord abundantly supplied grace to you? Name it and thank Him for it.

DAY FOUR
UNHOLY AMBITION

Pause. Breathe. Pray.

There are stories in the Bible I'm so glad the Lord included—human stories that remind me I'm not the only one (nor the first one) to go through a certain circumstance or struggle. The narrative in Numbers 16 is not one of those stories. It's bizarre and lacks any hint of the warm fuzzies. But it's in the canon of Scripture for a reason. We will dig in together to find one!

Read Numbers 16:1-40.

Who are the three men that assembled the group of two hundred fifty chiefs against Moses and Aaron? (Note their fathers and their tribe.)

_____ son of _____, son of _____, son of _____, with

_____ and _____, sons of _____ and

_____, son of _____, sons of _____.

According to Numbers 4, what were the sons of Kohath in charge of?

Look back at the diagrams of the arrangement of the tribes around the tabernacle (pp. 27,33). Where were the tribes of Reuben and the Kohathites?

What was the assembly's accusation against Moses and Aaron (v. 3)?

Was there a shred of truth in their accusation? If so, what was it?

Does anything about this smell fishy to you? The men's argument seemed reasonable and almost right. God had just instructed His people to put tassels on their garments to remind them of their calling to be His holy nation. Every one of His children was holy. However, there was a difference between their holiness as God's people and the holiness that accompanied the priesthood. God called His people to be His and to live according to His law. On the other hand, God chose the priests to approach His presence through offerings and sacrifices on behalf of the people. This was not the same thing.

Korah, Dathan, Abiram, and On took an almost true statement and built their argument around it. This has the sneaky fingerprints of the enemy all over it. Satan loves to take a truth and twist it just enough to make it a lie that will lead many astray. He did it in the garden of Eden with Adam and Eve (Gen. 3) and in the wilderness with Jesus (Matt. 4), although unsuccessfully. So why wouldn't he try it here?

> **Have you ever bought into a "twisted truth" that resulted in you being led astray?**

Another problem with Korah and Co.'s assertion became clearer when they accused Moses and Aaron of exalting themselves. Korah was Moses and Aaron's cousin. His father (Izhar) and Moses and Aaron's father (Amram) were brothers (Ex. 6:18). I wonder if there might have been some resentment and jealousy festering in Korah's heart. Maybe he thought: *If God chose Moses to lead the people and Aaron and his sons to serve as priests, why not me?* The Lord had chosen him, though, to do something pretty special. As a Kohathite, he and his brothers were in charge of carrying the most holy things: the ark of the covenant, the lampstand, and altars. These items were at the heart of the tabernacle. But for Korah, it wasn't enough.

Dathan, Abiram, and On were all of the tribe of Reuben. Their tents were basically in Korah's backyard. While Reuben was Jacob's firstborn son, his tribe was not placed in a prominent position around the tabernacle. The tribe of Judah occupied that spot. Maybe they were feeling a twinge of jealousy and resentment too. While we don't know specifically what motivated the men, we know that their twisted truth argument was an affront to the Lord.

I don't want to rush through this section without giving you (and myself!) an opportunity to search your heart for any jealousy or resentment.

As you read the previous paragraphs, did a situation or person come to mind? If so, take a moment to ask the Spirit to search your heart. Use this space to confess, give thanks for what He has given you, including His forgiveness, and ask Him to help you reframe your mind concerning this.

Look back at our text today and put the following in chronological order:

_____ Moses told Korah and his company that it is the Lord whom they sinned against.

_____ The Lord told Moses and Aaron to separate themselves from the congregation so that He may consume them, but Moses and Aaron interceded for the congregation.

_____ Fire consumed the two hundred fifty men offering incense.

_____ Dathan and Abiram refused to come up to Moses.

_____ Moses fell on his face and told Korah and all his company to take censers and offer incense before the Lord.

_____ The glory of the Lord appeared to all the congregation at the entrance of the tent of meeting.

_____ The ground swallowed up Korah and all who belonged to him.

_____ Moses told the people to separate themselves from the tents of Korah, Dathan, and Abiram.

Does this seem harsh to you? The *ESV Study Bible's* notes offer some clarification: "God executes swift judgment on those who thought they could assume the privileges of priesthood for themselves."[8]

Why is it significant that the Lord wanted Eleazar to take up the censers out of the blaze (vv. 37-40)?

The people of God needed tangible reminders of who they were and what they were to do, as well as who they were not and what they were not to do. The tassels prompted them to remember their holiness as God's people and the laws they were to obey for their flourishing and God's glory. The gold covering for the altar made from the two hundred fifty censers of unauthorized worship reminded them that, while they were holy, they were not designated to make offerings and sacrifices on their own behalf.

Questions running through Numbers 16 include: *What sort of ambition rules your heart? Is it a holy ambition—one like Moses and Aaron that is after God's glory and full surrender to His rule and reign? Or is it unholy ambition—one like Korah and his friends that is after one's own glory and fully committed to self-rule and self-reign?*

How would you answer those questions? (You're not alone if it's a little of both.)

James 4:6b says, "God opposes the proud but gives grace to the humble." God opposed Korah, Dathan, and Abiram. (It looks like On had enough sense to change his associations!) He gave grace to Moses and Aaron who did not lord their power and position over the others but humbly submitted themselves before the Lord, asking Him to declare who was right.

Notice that James 4:6b does not say, "God opposes the imperfect but gives grace to the perfect." Perfection doesn't require grace. If you answered the question above and felt some shame in your answer, may I encourage you? The first step in humility is admitting the truth of where you are. The next is to honestly cry out to God for forgiveness and help. His grace is sufficient for you.

For while we were still weak, at the right time Christ died for the ungodly. For one will scarcely die for a righteous person— though perhaps for a good person one would dare even to die—but God shows his love for us in that while we were still sinners, Christ died for us. Since, therefore, we have now been justified by his blood, much more shall we be saved by him from the wrath of God. For if while we were enemies we were reconciled to God by the death of his Son, much more, now that we are reconciled, shall we be saved by his life. More than that, we also rejoice in God through our Lord Jesus Christ, through whom we have now received reconciliation.

ROMANS 5:6-11

According to Romans 5:6-11, what state were we in when Christ died for us?

How is that comforting or encouraging to you?

We can only be loyal to one kingdom—ours or God's. When our hearts are set on our way and our glory (wanting everyone to make a big deal about us), we prove ourselves to be enemies of God's kingdom. Korah and the others were against God's kingdom, and they suffered His wrath. For those who believe in Christ, the earth won't swallow you up. Because of Jesus' death on the cross, we are rescued from the wrath of God. The only things that will be "swallow[ed] up" are death (Isa. 25:8) and the wrestle we have right now between loyalty to God's kingdom and ours (2 Cor. 5:4). When Christ returns, there will only be one King, and our hearts will freely rejoice under His reign.

DAY FIVE
AARON, GOD'S HIGH PRIEST

Pause. Breathe. Pray.

While we thought the grumbling would surely cease with the ground swallowing up Korah, Dathan, Abiram, and their people, and fire consuming the two hundred fifty men who offered incense, that sadly doesn't appear to be the case. Once again, we find God's people murmuring, and Moses and Aaron had front row seats to the whine fest. If nothing else, we have seen what these two men were made of. We have witnessed their humble submission to the Lord to serve Him by leading His people, no matter what. In today's study, we will see God show His power and mercy through His chosen servant Aaron.

Read Numbers 16:41-50.

When did the grumbling take place (v. 41)? Who grumbled? What was their charge, and who was it against (vv. 41-42)?

The glory of the Lord appeared outside the temple, and He gave some instructions to Moses and Aaron.

Do the Lord's words sound familiar? Where was the last time we heard these instructions?

How did Moses and Aaron respond (v. 45)?

What did Moses have Aaron do (v. 46)?

What form did the Lord's wrath take this time (vv. 47-49)?

What stopped the plague?

A STIFF-NECKED PEOPLE

In Exodus 32–34 the Lord repeatedly used the phrase "stiff-necked" to describe Israel. A synonym for *stiff-necked* is *obstinate*. Look up the term and write the definition here:

Our oldest daughter, Audrey, is a gifted equestrian. She caught the horse bug at age ten and hasn't recovered. She loves the challenge of channeling the power of a half-ton animal into an enjoyable experience for both horse and rider. I'm always amazed (and a little terrified) watching her round barrels at lightning speed. While Audrey herself is a force to be reckoned with, she has met her match a time or two. The temperament of the horse matters. Some horses take to the bit and bridle more easily than others. They trust and submit to their rider quickly. Others are more obstinate. It takes more time to build trust in order to train them. Some horses never make it past a certain point, either because the trainer gives up or the horse is too stubborn (or, sadly, was too traumatized by a bad trainer). These horses end up in pastures or as broodmares (baby-making female horses). The more submissive horses find jobs—racing around barrels, herding cows, carrying horseback riders— and they love it.

As humans, temperament plays a part in how we interact with others and with God, but we also have been given a heart to love certain things, a soul to long for eternity, a mind to reason and recognize right from wrong, and strength to choose between them. Will we submit our hearts to God to love the things He loves? Will we long for God to fill the eternal void in our souls? Will we set our minds on what is true, honorable, just, pure, lovely, commendable, excellent, and praiseworthy (Phil. 4:8)? Will we surrender our wills in order to obey God's? If we answer yes to these questions, we will know the joy that comes from a life fully submitted to God.

Imagine if Israel had just humbly received God's instructions without murmuring against Him. What could it have looked like?

Unfortunately, I can identify more with Israel's murmuring than Moses and Aaron's humble and merciful response or even Caleb and Joshua's faith-filled assurance in God's plan. Praise God there's Someone to intercede for me (and you) as Aaron interceded for the people.

At the end of Numbers 16, Moses instructed Aaron to offer incense to make atonement for the people. Unlike the two hundred fifty unauthorized men who offered incense before God, Aaron's offering was acceptable to the Lord. Instead of incurring the wrath of God, he satisfied it.

Obedience to God's Word is good and right, but without faith in Christ's atonement on our behalf, it's not enough to cover our sin. We cannot earn God's forgiveness. We can only receive it by believing that Christ's work is enough for us. Aaron was a shadow of the true form: Jesus. Where our offering is insufficient, Christ's is more than enough to satisfy God's wrath. Like Aaron, Christ stands between the living and the dead.

> And you were dead in the trespasses and sins in which you once walked, following the course of this world, following the prince of the power of the air, the spirit that is now at work in the sons of disobedience—among whom we all once lived in the passions of our flesh, carrying out the desires of the body and the mind, and were by nature children of wrath, like the rest of mankind. But God, being rich in mercy, because of the great love with which he loved us, even when **we were dead** in our trespasses, made us alive together with Christ—by grace you have been saved.
>
> EPHESIANS 2:1-5 (*emphasis mine*)

A time for reflection: after reading this section of the study, what stands out to you? Take a moment to write out some thoughts.

AARON: GOD'S CHOSEN PRIEST

Read Numbers 17.

What did the Lord want Moses to get from "each father's house" (v. 2)?

Where was Moses supposed to deposit the items (v. 4)?

According to verse 5, what was the desired result of this test?

What happened to Aaron's staff overnight (v. 8)?

What did the Lord have Moses do with Aaron's staff (vv. 9-11)?

How did the people respond to the test (vv. 12-13)?

In Numbers 17 we come to the last story in a series of three focused on the legitimacy of Aaron's priesthood. The first two started with the people grumbling and ended with God's wrath. The third story starts with the Lord speaking to Moses. He wanted to establish Aaron and his sons as priests proactively, not just in response to Israel's accusations.

The staffs were brought before the presence of the Lord (in front of the ark). Staffs from each of the tribes of Israel, plus Aaron's staff (representing the tribe of Levi) were there. Of the staffs, only Aaron's miraculously budded, blossomed, and produced fruit. This evidenced at least two things.

First, it proved to the people that Aaron and his sons were the only Israelites able to minister before the Lord as priests. Commentators don't know the significance of the almond, but most agree that "Their white blossoms symbolize purity, holiness, and God himself, which are all associated with the priesthood."[9] Aaron's staff was kept in front of the ark as a physical reminder to God's people that only those whom God approves may approach Him (specifically here, the tribe of Levi and the priestly leadership of Aaron).

Second, the miraculous blossoming of Aaron's staff was a display of God's ability to bring life from death. The staff was a dead stick until it was brought into the Lord's presence and burst with new life. This sign was "an example of what this omnipotent God can do and, indeed, what he has been doing for his people as he delivered them from Egypt."[10]

For the sake of time, I will sum up Numbers 18 and 19. However, I encourage you to read through these two chapters before the end of this study. Surprising treasures wait beneath the surface if you're willing to plumb their depths!

Numbers 18 outlines the duties of the priests and Levites.

> Quiz time: what's the difference between the two—the priesthood and the Levites? (We covered this in Session Two's personal study.)

In verse 8 we see the Lord spoke directly to Aaron alone. Previously, the Lord had only spoken to Moses, who passed the message on to Aaron. This is yet another affirmation of Aaron's legitimate position as mediator between God and His people. The rest of chapter 18 outlines how the people's contributions to the Lord are partly used to support the priests, Levites, and their families.

Numbers 19 reiterates the reality that God's presence is incompatible with death, thus God's people must treat death, especially human death, with solemnity and earnestness. The Lord gave Moses and Aaron a recipe for cleansing water to be used to purify those who have touched or have been close to a dead body. The seriousness with which God's people were to treat death reflects the seriousness they were to have when approaching His presence.

The gravity of these commands serves as another reminder for us of how Korah, Dathan, and Abiram underestimated the seriousness of God's word and presumed upon their qualifications as holy to the Lord. They mistakenly assumed God's hierarchy imitated man's: Those at the top (or center) have special favor that leads to more power and less demands on their lives.

> That is the heart of the problem with Korah and the other Levitical leaders of the rebellion: they did not want to be subservient. But the reality is that any form of ministry is subservient at its very core. Ministry is to serve others in the name of Jesus Christ.[11]

Have you ever looked at someone in vocational ministry and wished to trade places with him or her? If so, why?

The Lord called Aaron and his sons to minister before His presence and gave them the grace to do so. He gave the Levites the task of handling the tabernacle and its items and the grace to do so. He gave the other tribes land, produce, and animals to contribute to the offerings, sacrifices, and sustenance of the tabernacle duties and the grace to do so. Everyone had (and has) a part to play. Each was holy to the Lord. It took all of them to willingly participate in keeping the commands of the Lord and enjoying His presence among them.

Close today (and this session!) by writing out Mark 9:35 and meditating on that truth. Ask the Lord to help you embrace it according to the way He has called and gifted you.

I've provided some discussion questions here to get the conversation started. Feel free to discuss what you learned throughout the week of study, ask any questions you may have, and share what God is teaching you.

DISCUSSION QUESTIONS

Our trust in the Lord is contingent upon our fear of the Lord. Do you fear man more than God sometimes? Why? How might that reflect whom you're trusting?

Read Jeremiah 17:7-8 aloud in your group. What would it look like in your life for you to be "a tree planted by water," (v. 8) flourishing with God as your source?

Trusting the Lord doesn't mean we don't have a detour, but it does mean that even the detours lead to the destination. How does that truth encourage you to obedience despite difficult circumstances? Are you experiencing a detour in your life right now? Tell your group about it so they can support you in it.

Teaching sessions available for purchase or rent at *LifeWay.com/WithUsInTheWilderness*

FOR THEIR GOOD

God brings him out of Egypt

and is for him like the horns of the wild ox;

he shall eat up the nations, his adversaries,

and shall break their bones in pieces

and pierce them through with his arrows.

NUMBERS 24:8

DAY ONE
FIRST, THE BAD NEWS

Pause. Breathe. Pray.

My grandmother had a motto (and even a sign to accompany it in her kitchen)—"Life is uncertain; eat dessert first!" While I love this adage when it comes to actually eating, I'd rather have a sweet ending in real life. If someone says to me, "I have good news and bad news. Which would you like to hear first?" I'm always the bad-news-first kind of person. Give me hope at the end!

Over the past three weeks, we have followed along with the Israelites as they journeyed from Sinai to Kadesh, up to the edge of the promised land, but not into it. This is the second travel narrative of God's people from Egypt to Canaan. The first is recorded in Exodus, from the Red Sea to Sinai. This week, we will follow along on the third journey from Kadesh to the plains of Moab.

The first two journeys started off with great hope and anticipation: the Egyptians were defeated; the Red Sea parted; the cloud of fire led the way to the promised land, and the people looked to God's man, Moses, as their fearless leader. Then, they hit some speed bumps. The people complained of the lack of food and water; the spies came back with an unfavorable report, and the settlement in the promised land was postponed due to the people's lack of faith. On the third journey, however, the pattern was flipped. Numbers 20 starts with the bad news.

Read Numbers 20.

What are five "bad news items" that occurred in this chapter? (I've given you hints for each one.)

1. _____ (v. 1).

2. _____ (vv. 2-3).

3. _____ (vv. 10-12).

4. _____ (vv. 18-21).

5. _____ (v. 28).

Bad news is part of living in a broken world. Suffering is no respecter of age, occupation, class, or wealth. The people we love die, either by natural causes or unnatural. Our heroes fall. We succumb to temptation and sin against God and others. No one escapes bad news. The good news, however, is that Jesus came to save sinners (1 Tim. 1:15) and to bring His kingdom on earth. But we aren't living in the fullness of it yet. When He returns, all will be made completely right. For those who have put all their faith in Jesus, they will have no more suffering, no more death, no more struggle with sin. Even the earth will be made new.

Have you been hit with bad news lately? Does the good news of Jesus bring you any comfort? (If you feel comfortable sharing, let your friends or Bible study group know how they can be praying for you in the midst of bad news.)

THE DEATH OF MIRIAM

Miriam is the central female character in the exodus story. She is Moses' big sister who watched over him as their mother laid him in a basket and set him along the riverbank with the hope of saving his life (Ex. 2:2-3). She saw Pharaoh's daughter scoop him up out of the river. She shrewdly offered to find a Hebrew woman (her mother) to nurse baby Moses (vv. 4-10).

In Exodus 15 Miriam is called a "prophetess" (v. 20), and she led the women in a song: "Sing to the LORD, for he has triumphed gloriously; the horse and his rider he has thrown into the sea" (v. 21).

Yet Miriam was not a perfect spiritual superhero. Think back to Session Three of our study. What events recorded in Numbers 12 caused Miriam to be temporarily cast out of the Israelite camp?

Miriam died in the wilderness with the rest of God's people who refused to enter the promised land on His terms. Her death is a brief mention that occupies one sentence at the end of one verse. However, despite going out like a whimper, her legacy is preserved positively.

What did the prophet Micah write about Miriam in Micah 6:4?

How does this passage honor Miriam?

We all have our shining moments—the days we confidently boast in the God who we believe to be entirely able. And we all have our lackluster moments—the days we shake our fists at the heavens and question God's will for our lives. Miriam's legacy gives me hope that the Lord can redeem all my moments. I may suffer the consequences of my sin, but His mercy is enough to cover it, and His grace is enough to give me a legacy of faith.

Does Miriam's story give you hope? Are there moments that haunt you?

What about you? What do you hope your legacy will be?

THE WATERS OF MERIBAH

The Bible has two accounts of the people of Israel in need of water and the Lord providing through a rock. The first is in Exodus 17, and the second is here in Numbers 20. Some scholars believe they are two versions of the same story, but most believe they are two different accounts.[1]

Revisit Numbers 20:2-13.

What was the assembly's complaint (v. 5)?

How did Moses and Aaron respond (v. 6)?

What did the Lord tell Moses to do (v. 8)?

The Lord's patient endurance with His people is astounding. They grumbled and quarreled with Moses and Aaron—again. Yet His anger didn't burn against them. Despite their constant complaining, murmuring, and rebellion, the Lord had preserved His people and His promise. He instructed Moses to use Aaron's staff, the one that miraculously put forth leaves, blooms, and almonds, to show His unparalleled ability to come through for His people.

Why do you think the Lord wanted him to use Aaron's staff?

MOSES STRUCK THE ROCK

All seemed to be going according to plan: the people grumbled; Moses and Aaron fell on their faces before the tent of meeting; the Lord gave instructions; Moses and Aaron obeyed completely. Or did they?

To what was Moses supposed to speak (v. 8)? To whom did he speak instead (v. 10)?

What did Moses do with the staff (v. 11)? How did this differ from the Lord's instructions (v. 8)?

Did the rock produce water (v. 11)?

What were the consequences to Moses' actions (v. 12)?

Why do you think the consequences were so severe?

This moment might be the most tragic of all in Numbers. Up to this point, Moses had endured every leadership challenge and remained faithful, even if by the skin of his teeth, at times. It appears he had reached his limit. At this moment in the narrative, the people had wandered almost forty years. Forty years of manna. Forty years of grumbling. Forty years of following a cloud of fire from campsite to campsite—breaking down tents and the tabernacle, hauling people, cattle, and personal belongings over miles and miles of inhospitable wilderness. I can't really blame Moses for coming to the end of his rope. Yet the Lord requires "long obedience in the same direction."[2]

When Moses struck the rock instead of speaking to it, he committed the same sin of unbelief (and thus disobedience) that the people who trusted the spies' unfavorable report over the Lord's promise committed. Thus, Aaron and Moses' sentences were the same. They would not enter the promised land either.

A little spoiler: while Moses did not enter the promised land with the people, he did not fall out of fellowship with God.

What do Matthew 17:1-3 and Mark 9:1-4 say about Moses?

How does Hebrews 11:23-28 describe Moses?

Like his sister Miriam, Moses was a fallible human whom the Lord chose to use in profound ways. Although Moses lived hundreds of years before Christ came to earth, Romans 3:23-25 tells us that Jesus' blood satisfied God's holy anger against sin. "God looked forward to the cross of Christ where the full payment for the guilt of sin would be made, where Christ would die in the place of sinners."[3] The sacrifices in Numbers were a shadow pointing to the true form. By the blood of Jesus, the ultimate Passover Lamb, Moses is saved and enjoys uninhibited communion with the Lord—no grumbling, no falling on his face because of the people's murmuring. Instead, he stands in awe of the presence of God.

EDOM REFUSES PASSAGE

The Edomites were Israel's distant cousins. Jacob (later named Israel) had a twin brother named Esau. According to Genesis 36:1, the Edomites were Esau's descendants. This might explain why Moses dealt gently with them by sending a diplomatic letter as opposed to a show of force.

How did the Edomites respond (vv. 18-21)?

Does something seem to be missing here? I almost didn't catch the missing piece. Maybe it's because I am guilty of this strategy—making a plan without consulting the Lord or hitting a wall without asking the Lord for help. Nowhere in verses 14-21 do we see Moses ask the Lord for counsel or help. He just forged onward and side-stepped Edom when it didn't work out. This resulted in a major detour. They had to turn away from the promised land to go around Edom.

Is there a circumstance in your life right now in which you have failed to consult the Lord or ask Him for help? Ask Him. Write down whatever comes to mind.

Let's imagine Moses did entreat the Lord and the writer of Numbers omitted the conversation. Describe what Moses may have thought/felt when Edom refused passage.

Have you faced major detours on the way to something you felt the Lord had promised you?

I am always comforted by Psalm 139:3, "You search out my path and my lying down and are acquainted with all my ways." Although I might be surprised by the detours, the Lord never is. He knows. He is well acquainted with all my ways. He never loses track of His children.

AARON'S DEATH

Revisit Numbers 20:22-29.

The last of the bad news is an episode that carries tremendous significance. Aaron was the first high priest of Israel, thus his retirement and death are noteworthy.

> Locate Mount Hor (the one near Edom) on the map (p. 224). Draw a line from Kadesh Barnea to Mount Hor. (Your map has two mentions of Mount Hor. Some scholars believe two mountains shared that name.)[4]

> What phrase did the Lord use to refer to Aaron's death (v. 24)?

> Why was Aaron not allowed to enter the promised land (v. 24)?

> What did the Lord tell Moses to do to Aaron and Eleazar (vv. 25-26)?

> Where did Aaron die (v. 28)?

The phrase, "gathered to his people," was used "to describe the death of a righteous man in a ripe old age."[5] Abraham, Ishmael, Isaac, Jacob, and Moses were all "gathered to their people." We see that although Aaron was not allowed to enter the promised land, he was still considered a righteous man in the eyes of the Lord.

It was the end of an era. Three men walked to the top of Mount Hor and only two came down—one of whom wore his father's priestly clothes. The people mourned for thirty days, twenty-three more days than what was typical.[6]

My husband, Matt, preached a sermon in 2015 that included a phrase I can't forget: "The man goes into the ground, but the message goes on." In other words, the vessel (man or woman) the Lord chooses to use doesn't last forever, but the good news he or she shares about Christ does. Aaron died on top of a mountain and was gathered to his people. But the priesthood continued through his son, Eleazar. The Lord can use people in our lives that seem indispensable, but it's actually His Spirit within them and the message of the gospel that we can't live without.

> Take a moment as we close today to thank God for someone He has used in your life. Identify the characteristics in his or her life that look like Him.

DAY TWO
THINGS ARE LOOKING UP

Pause. Breathe. Pray.

Yesterday, we started with the bad news—Miriam's and Aaron's deaths, Moses' rebellion, and the Edomites' refusal to let Israel pass through their land. Today, however, we get to the good news (with a little more whining and subsequent judgment thrown in for good measure).

DEVOTED TO DESTRUCTION

Read Numbers 21:1-13.

Who instigated the conflict between Arad and Israel (v. 1)?

How did Israel respond (v. 2)?

How is this response different from the Israelites' response to Edom?

What was the result of the conflict (v. 3)?

What did they call the place (v. 3)?

This wasn't the first time the Israelites faced a difficult foe. Their cousins in Edom were anything but hospitable. Yet Israel's response to conflict and distress with Arad varied greatly from that with Edom. I can't help but wonder if Arad's offensive attack and capture of some of the Israelites prompted God's people to cry out for help more quickly. Personally, I am much more apt to pray for God's intervention in a situation when I feel the most powerless. Perhaps the Israelites felt more powerless against Arad than they did against Edom.

Is this true for you too? Do you tend to cry out for the Lord's help more when you feel the most powerless?

One of the reasons the Old Testament can be difficult to reconcile with the New Testament is seeing passages like Numbers 21:1-3 and the utter destruction that God's people bring to a whole city or group of people. This hardly sounds like they're turning the other cheek (Matt. 5:39). What's going on here?

I appreciated Gordon J. Wenham's insight on this passage:

> Deuteronomy justifies this treatment of the Canaanites as a preventive against apostasy (7:4). Brutal as it seems to us, it is of a piece with the rest of Israel's penal code, which insists on the death penalty for a wide range of religious offences. Fidelity to the LORD and the purity of the faith ranked highest of the values in Israel's ethical and religious system.[7]

For Israel, faithfulness to the Lord and purity of faith looked like obeying the Lord's commands to "devote them to complete destruction" (Deut. 7:2). If the Israelites left the people living in Canaan alone, they would be setting themselves up for the temptation to be led astray. This is not unlike Christians' radical call to remove stumbling blocks from our path. Jesus told His followers to cut off a hand or foot or tear out an eye if any such part caused them to sin (Mark 9:43-48). While He was being hyperbolic, He was communicating the seriousness with which we should take temptation in our lives. We are not meant to keep them around like pets. Temptations are untamable.

Is there a temptation in your life that, until now, you have tolerated but haven't fully rejected? If so, what could it look like to "cut it off" or devote it to utter destruction?

THE CURIOUS CASE OF THE COPPER SERPENT

Read Numbers 21:4-9.

Why do you think the people became impatient?

Is their complaint familiar? Was it true?

What was the "worthless food" (v. 5)?

What form did God's judgment take this time?

What was the people's confession?

What did Moses do in response? What did the Lord tell him to do?

I loathe inefficiency, especially when driving. Even if I know a route might be faster, if it starts out in the opposite direction of my destination, I just can't do it. (Can I get a witness?) Israel found themselves going the long way around because of Edom's opposition. The Israelites' impatience with the detour seemed to make them more prone to irritability. If things weren't bad enough, they had to endure this worthless food! No water! They were as good as dead! Or were they? I distinctly remember the Lord providing water from a rock. If He could manage that, I'm pretty sure He could meet their needs. And the worthless food? Did you mean the manna and quail that miraculously appeared every morning for gathering and consumption? Oh yeah, that? There are descriptors that might fit more accurately—*redundant* or *bland*—but definitely not *worthless*.

As much as I want to criticize the Israelites' complaining, I can see too much of myself in them. I'm "all in" at the start of a project or adventure, but when things get uncomfortable or downright difficult, I start seeing (and naming!) all the problems.

Can you relate?

This time, the Lord's judgment took the shape of fiery serpents. It is doubtful that the serpents were literally fiery. What's more likely is that their bites burned like fire, and they may have been shiny and reddish in color. More important than the serpents' appearance was their symbolism. Ancient Egyptian texts featured stories of fiery serpents protecting Pharaoh and Egypt.[8] They were emblems of Egypt. The people thought that relief and salvation would be found in Egypt. Instead, the Lord showed the inevitable destruction that comes from trusting in anything or anyone besides the Lord. The pain caused by the serpents' fatal bites provoked the people to come to their senses. They admitted their sin and implored Moses to pray for them.

How has the Lord used painful circumstances to help you see your sin and draw you back to Him?

The antidote to Israel's trouble came in a similar form to the trouble itself. The Lord told Moses to fashion a serpent out of copper and fix it onto a pole. Those who had been bitten were to look at the copper serpent and be healed. Gordon J. Wenham notes that the remedy here is in line with others like it in the Old Testament. For example, the purification requirements for those who were made unclean by blood involved blood being spilled (through animal sacrifice). Also, the ashes of a dead heifer were mixed in water used to cleanse those who had touched a dead body (Num. 19). This makes sense, then, that "Those inflamed and dying through the bite of living snakes were restored to life by a dead reddish-coloured snake."[9]

In John 3:14-15 Jesus shed light on the incident of the copper serpent.

> *And as Moses lifted up the serpent in the wilderness, so must the Son of Man be lifted up, that whoever believes in him may have eternal life.*

Compare and contrast Numbers 21:9 and John 3:14-15.

Jesus wasn't lifted up on a pole, but He was lifted up on a cross. His life is a judgment on humanity. He lived the perfect life we could never live. He died the death we deserved. He told us that holiness and right-standing before God cannot be achieved by our own strength. He preached that our righteousness must exceed that of the most righteous religious leaders of His day. By all accounts, we are doomed. But the form of judgment is also the form of our salvation. Like Israel, we look to the form for redemption and atonement. For Israel, it was the copper serpent. For us, it is Christ. We "fix our eyes on Jesus, the author and perfecter of our faith, who for the joy set before Him endured the cross, scorning its shame, and sat down at the right hand of the throne of God" (Heb. 12:2, BSB).

If you need to take a praise break (a moment to just thank the Lord for His kindness and provision), do so here. Write out your prayer of thanks below.

ISRAEL IS ON A ROLL

Read Numbers 21:10-35.

There's an old western theme song from the show *Rawhide* that I can't get out of my head as I read this next section of Scripture. It's a cattle-driving song that encourages the singers and listeners to keep pushing the herd home where loved ones await. The lyrics say:

Rollin', Rollin', Rollin',

Though the streams are swollen

Keep them doggies rollin'

Rawhide[10]

I'm not sure whose hide is raw, but either way, the temporary discomfort is worth the hard push toward the destination.

After wandering in the wilderness for nearly forty years, Israel was in her final push toward the promised land. The end of Numbers 21 is filled with conquests and songs. The end was finally in sight.

What provision did the people sing about in verse 18?

The encounter with King Sihon was similar to Edom. What was the difference in the outcome (v. 24)?

Who came out against Israel in verse 33?

How does chapter 21 conclude?

Things were indeed starting to look up for Israel. It was a bumpy start, but the Israelites were at last rolling their doggies along, songs and all. Though they lacked faith, the Lord did not lack in faithfulness. He kept His presence among them and brought them into the land He promised.

Close by reading Psalm 100 and thanking God for His faithfulness to all generations.

DAY THREE
THE UNLIKELY PROPHET

Pause. Breathe. Pray.

The whole reason you are holding this study in your hand is due, in part, to Numbers 22. A few years ago, I received a copy of the *She Reads Truth* Bible. (It's a beautiful Bible with insightful devotionals interspersed throughout.) I had read Genesis and Exodus, perused Deuteronomy and Leviticus, but I had yet to fully tackle Numbers. This Bible was so aesthetically pleasing that even the cover page for Numbers grabbed my attention. I was surprised to find so much with which I could relate in this book of the Bible. But it was the humorous and peculiar story of the prophet Balaam that sealed the deal. I had so many questions about his interaction with the Lord and Israel. Was he a false prophet or a true prophet? Was he on God's side or on Moab's side? Why did God seem to communicate two different things at the same time? We may not be able to find all of our answers to these questions, but we will at least try!

Read Numbers 22.

BALAAM'S DIARY

You may have noticed during our study together that we have established somewhat of a pattern of reading chunks of Scripture and then answering questions about the content. Today, we will change it up a bit.

Verses 2-35 narrate the span of three to four days. In the "journal" on the next page, write out what you think Balaam would have written in his diary for that day. (I've filled out the first day for you.)

Day One (vv. 2-8)

Today, Balak (the King of Moab), sent messengers of Moab and Midian to me. He had a lot of nice things to say about me (and money too!), but that's not why he called. Apparently, a savage group of people named Israel is camped out in Moab and causing a stir. Balak wants me to come to him and speak curses on these people. I told them to stay the night, and I would get back with them in the morning. We will see what the Lord says tonight.

Day Two (vv. 9-14)

Day Three (vv. 15-19)

Day Four (vv. 20-35)

I know your hand might be getting tired (you just wrote three days' worth of diary entries!) but bear with me.

What are some questions you had as you read the text?

An important rule in interpreting Scripture is letting Scripture interpret itself. This means we look to other parts of the Bible that speak into or shed light on the part you are trying to understand.

How does 2 Peter 2:15 characterize Balaam?

According to the rest of Scripture, Balaam's motives were not as pure as they seem in Numbers 22. He is characterized as a man who was ultimately after financial gain. He wasn't on Team Balak nor Team Yahweh. He was number one on the roster for Team Balaam. A false prophet doesn't necessarily prophesy false information. They can prophesy something true but with impure motives or the intent to lead the hearers astray.

> **Do we have false prophets today? How can we discern between false prophets and godly teachers?**

A DONKEY BECOMES A PROPHET

> **Read Numbers 22:22-41.**

In Balaam's last encounter with the Lord at night, the Lord seemed to change His mind about Balaam and the princes of Moab. Unlike the first encounter, the Lord allowed Balaam to go with them, but He emphasized that Balaam should only speak what the Lord told him to speak. So which is it? Should Balaam go or should he not? God made His intentions clear to Balaam as he was on his way to Balak.

> **Look back at the passage. How many times did Balaam's donkey see the angel of the Lord?**

> **How did the donkey respond to the first sighting (v. 23)? How did Balaam respond?**

> **How did the donkey respond to the second sighting (v. 25)? How did Balaam respond?**

> **How did the donkey respond to the third sighting (v. 27)? How did Balaam respond?**

Each time, Balaam struck his donkey in response to her unusual behavior. Finally, the Lord opened her mouth, and she called Balaam out for hitting her when all she was trying to do was save his life! The Lord eventually opened the "all-powerful" prophet's eyes (sarcasm!) to see the angel of the Lord standing in the way with a sword in his hand. He condemned Balaam's mission but allowed him to go and only speak the Lord's words.

We will read more about this tomorrow, but the donkey was prophetically demonstrating what would happen when Balaam tried to speak curses over Israel at Balak's request. He made three attempts to curse Israel, but the Lord opposed them all.

Balak made a statement about Balaam that was actually more true about Israel: "he whom you bless is blessed, and he whom you curse is cursed" (v. 6).

What does Genesis 12:3 say about this?

Israel was on the cusp of entering the promised land. The Israelites had been tearing through the other nations in a victory march. The enemies of God and His people were intent on stopping them. What they didn't realize is that the Lord can use anything for His purposes. In this case, He used a donkey to speak. The prophet paid to speak curses would only be able to utter blessings. This would only increase Israel's confidence that the Lord would come through for her.

As Christians, we don't wrestle against earthly kings, insecure leaders, or opportunistic prophets, "but against the rulers, against the authorities, against the cosmic powers over this present darkness, against the spiritual forces of evil in the heavenly places" (Eph. 6:12b). The enemy has a plan for our lives: "to steal and kill and destroy" us (John 10:10). But the Lord has a greater plan, and He will use whatever it takes to fulfill it. He took the curse of the cross and turned it into a blessing for anyone who would receive Him. He can take whatever might be hanging over your head or weighing on your heart and use it to draw you nearer to Him.

In closing, take a minute to ask Him to do this for you.

DAY FOUR
A RISING STAR

Pause. Breathe. Pray.

Picture it. The tents of Israel spread out along the banks of the Jordan River in the plains of Moab, mere miles from the promised land. Above the thousands of tents spaced evenly and deliberately according to the four cardinal directions rose a larger tent, the tabernacle, placed exactly at the camp's center. Men, women, and children shuffled between the tents, going about their day like every day of the last forty years. They looked to the heart of the camp to see if anything had changed. Would they move forward today? Would this be the last day in the wilderness?

On one of the hilltops surrounding them, unknown to Israel, the king of Moab and his hired prophet Balaam attempted to bring down curses on the Israelites' camp. But as if there was a canopy of grace covering their dwellings, the curses slipped through and became blessings. While Israel had no clue that a divine exchange was taking place, the Lord remained faithful to His promise to keep Israel as His own. He put His words in the prophet's mouth and allowed him to catch a glimpse of God's glorious plan for His people.

Read Numbers 22:41–24:25.

Compare the first two oracles using the chart below.

	FIRST ORACLE	SECOND ORACLE
Location given		
Ceremony attached to the oracle		
To whom was the oracle given?		
What were the main points of the oracle?		

The process of building the altars and offering seven bulls and seven rams was a typical divination ritual in the ancient Near East. It was an attempt to entice the gods to do one's bidding.[11] Balak wanted to enlist Balaam to use God on his behalf, but Yahweh would not be used. He is not like other fickle "gods" who are hard to please and dwell on mountaintops or in the sky or in the depths of the sea. He is steadfast, faithful, and dwells among His people.

THE ORACLES

As you read through the oracles again, underline phrases that sound familiar. Circle terms that are unfamiliar. After each oracle, I will expound on a few items within it. For the most part, I want this to be an exercise where you do some digging too. Feel free to look up the cross-references in your Bible (the superscript letters and numbers at the end of words and verses), as well as use some commentaries online.

BALAAM'S FIRST ORACLE (23:7b-10)

From Aram Balak has brought me,
    the king of Moab from the eastern mountains:
"Come, curse Jacob for me,
    and come, denounce Israel!"
How can I curse whom God has not cursed?
    How can I denounce whom the LORD has not denounced?
For from the top of the crags I see him,
    from the hills I behold him;
behold, a people dwelling alone,
    and not counting itself among the nations!
Who can count the dust of Jacob
    or number the fourth part of Israel?
Let me die the death of the upright,
    and let my end be like his!

Hopefully some of Balaam's references sounded familiar. We covered some of these ideas in Session Two—in particular: the Lord changing Jacob's name to Israel and promising Abraham that the number of his descendants would be vast (like stars or, here, dust). The "people dwelling alone, and not counting itself among the nations!" refers to Israel's holiness—that the Israelites are a people set apart for God's glory.

How did Balak respond to Balaam's first oracle?

BALAAM'S SECOND ORACLE (vv. 18b-24)

Rise, Balak, and hear;
    give ear to me, O son of Zippor:
God is not man, that he should lie,
    or a son of man, that he should change his mind.
Has he said, and will he not do it?
    Or has he spoken, and will he not fulfill it?
Behold, I received a command to bless:
    he has blessed, and I cannot revoke it.
He has not beheld misfortune in Jacob,
    nor has he seen trouble in Israel.
The Lord their God is with them,
    and the shout of a king is among them.
God brings them out of Egypt
    and is for them like the horns of the wild ox.
For there is no enchantment against Jacob,
    no divination against Israel;
now it shall be said of Jacob and Israel,
    "What has God wrought!"
Behold, a people! As a lioness it rises up
    and as a lion it lifts itself;
it does not lie down until it has devoured the prey
    and drunk the blood of the slain.

Balak believed that maybe he got their location wrong. He thought if they just moved over to another mountain with a better vantage point, the Lord would heed their requests. Although Balaam already knew the outcome, he still went along with Balak's plan.

Why do you think he did that?

What did Balaam rebuke about Balak in this second oracle?

Verse 7 in Psalm 32 (a psalm of David) resonates with this oracle.

> *You are a hiding place for me; you preserve me from trouble; you surround me with shouts of deliverance.*

Although the Israelites had no idea Balaam was high above their heads attempting to pronounce curses on them, the Lord protected and preserved them. He surrounded them with shouts of deliverance in the spiritual realm that their human ears could not hear.

BALAAM'S THIRD ORACLE (24:3b-9)

The oracle of Balaam the son of Beor,
    the oracle of the man whose eye is opened,
the oracle of him who hears the words of God,
    who sees the vision of the Almighty,
    falling down with his eyes uncovered:
How lovely are your tents, O Jacob,
    your encampments, O Israel!
Like palm groves that stretch afar,
    like gardens beside a river,
like aloes that the LORD has planted,
    like cedar trees beside the waters.
Water shall flow from his buckets,
    and his seed shall be in many waters;
his king shall be higher than Agag,
    and his kingdom shall be exalted.
God brings him out of Egypt
    and is for him like the horns of the wild ox;
he shall eat up the nations, his adversaries,
    and shall break their bones in pieces
    and pierce them through with his arrows.
He crouched, he lay down like a lion

and like a lioness; who will rouse him up?
Blessed are those who bless you,
and cursed are those who curse you.

Did you find the water imagery ironic? One of the most common complaints among the people of Israel was about the lack of it! Here, though, they are likened to gardens beside a river and cedars trees beside the waters with water flowing from their buckets. Water is the source of life. We cannot exist without it.

In John 4 Jesus sat with a woman at a well. He explained to her that He is able to give her "living water" (v. 10) that would be "a spring of water welling up to eternal life" (v. 14). The promise in Numbers 24 foreshadows the Messiah, Jesus, who would come from Israel and be the King "higher than Agag" (v. 7).

BALAAM'S FINAL ORACLE (vv. 15b-24)

For the final oracle, Balak and Balaam were still at the spot where he gave the third. They could see Israel camping tribe by tribe. Balaam told Balak what the future held in store for Israel and her enemies.

The oracle of Balaam the son of Beor,
the oracle of the man whose eye is opened,
the oracle of him who hears the words of God,
and knows the knowledge of the Most High,
who sees the vision of the Almighty,
falling down with his eyes uncovered:
I see him, but not now;
I behold him, but not near:
a star shall come out of Jacob,
and a scepter shall rise out of Israel;
it shall crush the forehead of Moab
and break down all the sons of Sheth.
Edom shall be dispossessed;
Seir also, his enemies, shall be dispossessed.
Israel is doing valiantly.
And one from Jacob shall exercise dominion

and destroy the survivors of cities!
Then he looked on Amalek and took up his discourse and said,
"Amalek was the first among the nations,
but its end is utter destruction."
And he looked on the Kenite, and took up his discourse and said,
"Enduring is your dwelling place,
and your nest is set in the rock.
Nevertheless, Kain shall be burned
when Asshur takes you away captive."
And he took up his discourse and said,
"Alas, who shall live when God does this?
But ships shall come from Kittim
and shall afflict Asshur and Eber;
and he too shall come to utter destruction."

The star and scepter rising out of Israel was a prophecy about the dynasty of King David who would defeat Israel's enemies, including Moab. However, King David was the shadow of the true form—King Jesus. All of Scripture, from Numbers to 1 and 2 Kings and beyond, point to Jesus.

Though He couldn't have known it, as Balaam prophesied about the destruction of Israel's enemies, He was foretelling the gospel. In Jesus' death and resurrection, the enemies of God's people—sin, death, and Satan—were defeated.

While we don't see the full effects of His victory now, we will see them when He returns.

As Christians, we are adopted into God's family. If we are not ethnically Jewish, we still get to enjoy the blessing of Israel. Through Christ, the King who arose as a star and scepter from among Israel, all the nations are blessed. The blessings spoken over Israel are true for us.

Only God knows the full extent of the protection He has provided for His children. Like Israel, we could be totally oblivious to the perils above our heads. However, we can trust the Lord to do good and to be faithful to His Word.

> **Close today's study by writing out Psalm 91:1-6 in a journal and thank the Lord He promises to protect you, even against enemies you cannot see.**

DAY FIVE
ISRAEL TAKES A TUMBLE

Pause. Breathe. Pray.

My high school had a large bank of stairs right in the middle of the busiest section of school. Kids poured up, down, around, and through it between classes. Every day of all my years there, I feared making a misstep and tumbling to my (social) death in front of the entire school. Miraculously, I managed to stay upright through my senior year, but an unlucky few did not have the same experience. Their falls were announced through notes and conversations in the halls within a matter of moments. (Praise God the smartphone hadn't been invented yet—or there surely would have been video evidence!)

As we finish this week's study, we will see that just when it looked like the Israelites were hitting their stride, they tripped up on their own feet. In light of the previous blessings announced over them by Balaam, the heights from which they fell were quite spectacular.

Read Numbers 25.

Where were the Israelites living (v. 1)?

What did the people begin to do (v. 1)?

What did this act lead to (v. 2)?

What god did the Israelites yoke themselves to (v. 3)?

In response, what did the Lord tell Moses to do (v. 4)? What did Moses do (v. 5)?

What brazen act did one Israelite commit (v. 6)?

Who stopped the plague? How (vv. 7-9)?

God's people were living in the last encampment before they crossed the Jordan into the promised land. They could practically smell the milk and honey. But right there with the promises of God were the distractions and temptations of the world. In this case, it was prostitution in Moab that led to worship of the Moabites' god, Baal of Peor.

Are you starting to see a pattern here? The heights of God's blessings on His people (through Balaam) are juxtaposed with Israel's blatant sin. Scripture brings "home to us the full wonder of God's grace in face of man's incorrigible propensity to sin."[12] Think back to Moses coming down from Mount Sinai to see the people worshiping the golden calf. The revelation of God was followed up with Israel's idolatry. In fact, there are several parallels between what happened at Sinai and what happened here in the plains of Moab.

Fill in the parallel events.

SINAI	PLAINS OF MOAB
Moses was given revelation from God (Ex. 24–31).	Balaam spoke blessings over Israel (Num. 23–24).
The people worshipped the golden calf (Ex. 32).	
The Levites slaughtered the guilty (Ex. 32:25-28).	
The tribe of Levi was set apart for service in the tabernacle (Ex. 32:29).	

Not much has changed about God's people. We can still go from worshiping the Living God to bowing down to our idols in a blink of an eye. Even this morning, after a time of prayer, Bible study, and a sweet family devotion, I got into my car and was immediately perturbed by other drivers. I went from the heights of pure communion with the Lord to the depths of self-centeredness and self-righteousness within a matter of minutes.

Have you experienced something like this?

THE SERIOUSNESS OF SIN

This shocking episode graphically illustrates a truth summed up perfectly by theologian John Owen, "be killing sin or it will be killing you."[13]

Sin is not our friend. It may feel good at first. It may seem like no big deal, but it will kill us. James 1:14-15 fleshes it out.

But each person is tempted when he is lured and enticed by his own desire. Then desire when it has conceived gives birth to sin, and sin when it is fully grown brings forth death.

JAMES 1:14-15

God isn't trying to ruin your fun; He is saving your life. Just as we have seen Israel vacillate between faithfulness and faithlessness, we are prone to do the same. We bask in the glory of the mountain highs only to find ourselves tumbling back toward the plains of Moab.

We are not without hope, though. Jesus came to atone for our sin and to give us His righteousness. Not only that, He left us His Spirit to help us in our weakness (Rom. 8:26). Unlike the Israelites, we have the Holy Spirit living inside us. He is our Helper (John 14:16,26; 15:26; 16:7). He is with us forever. (John 14:16). He teaches all things and brings to remembrance all that Jesus taught. He bears witness about Jesus (Rom. 8:16). This means when we bear witness about Jesus, who He is and what He's done, the Holy Spirit is working through us. He intercedes on our behalf when we are all out of words (Rom. 8:26). His fruit, love, joy, peace, patience, kindness, goodness, faithfulness, gentleness, and self-control, is borne in our lives when we surrender to His will (Gal. 5:22-23).

We are not resigned to fall from the heights and stay there. By the Spirit, we are able to get back up and keep going.

Write Romans 8:1-4 below.

How do these verses give you hope in your battle with sin?

God knew we couldn't maintain the heights, so He made a way through His Son, Jesus. Jesus fulfilled the Law. He maintained faithfulness. If we believe Him for this, we get to walk according to His Spirit. We may take a tumble or two, but He will be there to pick us up and let us try again.

This has been a full week with a lot of bad news but even more good news.

To close, take a moment and pray for God to help you agree with Him that sin is deadly serious, turn from sin, and run to Him.

I've provided some discussion questions here to get the conversation started. Feel free to discuss what you learned throughout the week of study, ask any questions you may have, and share what God is teaching you.

DISCUSSION QUESTIONS

How does understanding Jesus' sacrifice on the cross to free you from sin and death affect the way you live your everyday life? Are there areas where you might need to shift your perspective?

In times of pain and hardship, it can be difficult to focus on God's presence with us because the hurt is so real. How might you encourage a friend or counsel your own heart to turn to God in those tough seasons?

God doesn't waste our suffering. He uses it for our good. Does that encourage you to keep going in a situation that might feel difficult? Is it hard for you to believe? Explain.

Teaching sessions available for purchase or rent
at *LifeWay.com/WithUsInTheWilderness*

A NEW GENERATION

The Lord spoke to Moses, saying, "Command the people of Israel and say to them, 'My offering, my food for my food offerings, my pleasing aroma, you shall be careful to offer to me at its appointed time.'"

NUMBERS 28:1-2

OUR PROMISE-KEEPING GOD

Pause. Breathe. Pray.

It's a new week and a whole new group of people along for the journey into the promised land. There are a couple of exceptions, but, for the most part, Israel was starting anew.

As we continue to read through Numbers, we will see the Lord is consistent. After the dark of night, the sun always rises in the east. After winter, spring is always there. He is the God of new beginnings. And He is the God who always keeps His promises—even if the way in which He keeps them doesn't look like what we had in mind.

THE NEW GENERATION

Read Numbers 26.

Compare the census from Numbers 1 with the census taken in Numbers 26 by filling in the population listed in Numbers 26 in column three.

TRIBE	NUMBERS 1	NUMBERS 26
Reuben	46,500	
Simeon	59,300	
Gad	45,650	
Judah	74,600	
Issachar	54,400	
Zebulun	57,400	

TRIBE	NUMBERS 1	NUMBERS 26
Manasseh	32,200	
Ephraim	40,500	
Benjamin	35,400	
Dan	62,700	
Asher	41,500	
Naphtali	53,400	

Who was to be counted according to Numbers 26:2?

How does Numbers 26:11 bring clarity to your understanding of what happened in Numbers 16?

How many Levites are listed in Numbers 3:39? In Numbers 26:62?

Why are the Levites not listed among the people of Israel (v. 62)?

Sum up Numbers 26:63-65 in your own words.

In Numbers 26 we get to the heart of why most people skip Numbers in their Bible reading plan. The list of seemingly random names and numbers lulls the average reader into a boredom-induced nap. Not so for us. (I hope!) These aren't just hard-to-pronounce names on pages. They're real people with real stories with whom we've started to become acquainted.

The Lord had Moses and Eleazar take another census for two reasons: for military purposes and apportioning land. A third reason runs underneath the other two: God's proof that He kept His promise to His people. While the population differences varied from tribe to tribe, there was only a variance of 1,820 people among the tribes and one thousand among the Levites.[1]

Despite constant complaining, murmuring, and rebellion, the Lord had preserved His people and His promise.

I am consistently overwhelmed with gratitude and incredulity when I think about God's faithfulness to me even when I have complained, murmured, and chosen my comfort and will over Him. He doesn't kick me out of His home. He doesn't disown me as His child. His love is constant and His promises are sure. Don't get me wrong, my sin has consequences. He may discipline me as His child. But because of Christ's death and resurrection, the worst consequence to sin—eternal separation from God—is off the table.

Romans 8:38-39 says:

> *For I am sure that neither death nor life, nor angels nor rulers, nor things present nor things to come, nor powers, nor height nor depth, nor anything else in all creation, will be able to separate us from the love of God in Christ Jesus our Lord.*

Can you relate? If so, how? If not, why?

THE LAND

We also see that the Lord was reasonable in apportioning the land. He gave larger pieces to larger tribes and smaller pieces to smaller tribes. As a parent, I can appreciate this approach, as well as the method of casting lots to decide which tribe inherited a specific piece of land. Casting lots was an unbiased and impartial way of making important decisions (much like the practice of flipping a coin at the beginning of a football game to determine who gets to choose starting field position). If I'd known about casting lots when my kids were younger, I would have incorporated this method when they fought over two halves of a cookie! I imagine the Lord was protecting Moses from playing patriarchal referee between the tribes. I also imagine Moses was incredibly grateful for it.

The Levites are listed separately because they were not meant to participate in military duties, nor would they receive portions of the land like the other tribes. Instead, they were set apart to perform their religious duties in and around the tabernacle. We will see in Numbers 35 that, though they were not given land, they were given cities within the other tribes' inheritance.

I don't know about you, but I struggled with the Levites' exemption from the land apportioning. To me, it didn't seem fair! As I've taken a closer look, though, I see that they had the privilege of participating in the manifestation of the Lord's presence among His people. They "got God" and "gave God." The Lord Himself was their inheritance and portion. The Levites' presence among each tribe's portion of land was a reminder of the Lord's presence with His people.

At the end of chapter 26, the writer of Numbers shows us that not only did God keep the warm, fuzzy, milk and honey promises we like, He also kept the promises we don't like.

Turn back to Numbers 14:28-30.

What promise did the Lord make that we see He kept in 26:64-65?

THE DAUGHTERS OF ZELOPHEHAD

Read Numbers 27:1-11.

Look back at Numbers 26. Where's the first place the daughters of Zelophehad are mentioned? To what tribe did they belong?

What request did they make (27:3-4)?

What did Moses do with their request (v. 5)?

How did the Lord respond to them (vv. 7-11)?

What do you think about the daughters of Zelophehad's request?

What does this story reveal about the character of God?

Before the daughters of Zelophehad are mentioned in the census in chapter 26, the last mention of *daughters* was in reference to the daughters of Moab and Israel's apostasy with them. The account of Mahlah, Noah[2] (spelled differently in Hebrew than Noah[3] who built the ark), Hoglah, Milcah, and Tirzah is a welcome departure from the previous story. These women were brave and confident that God would not only hear them, but that He would bring Israel into the land. If they weren't convinced that the Lord would fulfill His promise, then they had no reason to ask for an inheritance in the land. Their faith pleased the Lord. Their courage resulted in a new statute and rule for the people of Israel that would benefit families for generations to come.

Here's what we can say about God: He keeps His word. He is the promise-keeping God.

Maybe this truth gives you comfort because you are whole-heartedly relying on His grace to be sufficient for you. Maybe it causes you to wince because some of your hopes and dreams haven't panned out. It's easy to confuse what we want for our lives with what God wants. Sometimes we think a dream from our heart is a promise God has made to us. Yes, He can put dreams in our hearts for His purposes, but what's better than a dream fulfilled is an intimate relationship with the God of the universe. The best promise is not that all of our wishes come true, but that He will be with us no matter what (Matt. 28:20)—that absolutely nothing can separate us from His love.

> What's your response to the Lord's faithfulness? Are you grateful? Are you skeptical? Close today's personal study with a prayer of gratitude, confession, or a cry for His help and grace.

DAY TWO
JOSHUA

Pause. Breathe. Pray.

Today we will break from our regularly scheduled programming to take a deep dive into the study of one of the wilderness wanderers: Joshua. We'll start off surveying his life and end with what Numbers 27 reveals about him and a sneak peek into his future. I think you'll be glad we took this slight detour.

THE WARRIOR

The first mention of Joshua is found in Exodus 17:8-13. You might find this passage familiar. Usually the focus is less on Joshua and more on what is happening on the hill above him.

Read Exodus 17:8-13 and write a summary.

What role did Joshua play in these events?

THE ONE WHO WAITS

The next time we see Joshua in the pages of Scripture is in Exodus 24. The Lord told Moses to bring Aaron, his sons (Nadab and Abihu), and seventy elders to worship on Mount Sinai while Moses went up even nearer to the Lord. Once they arrived, the Lord appeared to them: "they beheld God, and ate and drank" (v. 11). They had a dinner party with the God of the universe! Can you imagine? Then Moses went up even further, but he wasn't alone. Joshua went with him.

In Exodus 24:13 what was Joshua called?

Before Moses and Joshua had made the trip further up the mountain, Moses gave instructions to the elders. He told them to wait there for him and to look to Aaron and Hur to settle any disputes that might arise while he was gone. We can assume from the text that Joshua did not enter the cloud of God's presence with Moses but must have stayed outside the cloud, in-between Moses and Aaron and the elders.

> **According to Exodus 24:18, how long was Moses on the mountain with God?**

That was a long time to wait. While the elders waited together with Aaron and Hur, Joshua waited for Moses in solitude. I'm not sure I could have endured as long as Joshua did! In fact, we know that Aaron and the elders lacked the stamina. At some point they left their post, went back to camp, and helped the people build a golden calf to worship. Joshua, however, waited for Moses to return. As Moses and Joshua made their way down the mountain, it was Joshua who first heard the ruckus of rebellion—the people singing and dancing before the idol they had made.

> **What does this episode show us about Joshua?**

THE WORSHIPER

> **Read Exodus 33:7-11.**

> **Compare what the people did to what Joshua did.**

What did the people do when Moses was in the tent (v. 10)?	What did Joshua do when Moses was in the tent (v. 11)?

Write what this shows us about Joshua.

When I try to put myself in Joshua's shoes, I can only hope I would be as patient, loyal, enduring, and besotted with the presence of God. He didn't presume upon God's grace or his position as Moses' assistant and endeavor to enter the conversation with God at the tent with Moses. He accepted his place and worshiped the Lord right where he was. The fringes of the cloud of God's presence and the flaps of the tent of meeting were enough for him. He didn't challenge Moses' leadership like Korah, Abiram, Dathan, or even Aaron and Miriam. He fought battles for Moses. He waited patiently for Moses. He attended Moses. All without complaint or murmuring.

One story that you might recall from Numbers 11 reveals the humanity of Joshua. The Lord took some of the Spirit that was on Moses and put it on seventy elders. Word got to Joshua that two elders did not go to the tent to prophesy but started prophesying in the middle of the camp. Joshua told Moses about it and urged him to stop that nonsense. Moses replied with this question: "Are you jealous for my sake?" (v. 29).

From what you have learned so far about Joshua, what do you think the answer might have been?

Aside from this little chink in his armor, Joshua continued to prove himself faithful. When he and Caleb returned from spying out the land, they were the only voices of reason and hope. They believed the people of Israel would be empowered by the Lord to take the land that God had promised to them. It was because of their faith in this moment that they were the only men of the first generation allowed to enter the promised land.

THE SUCCESSOR

Let's pick the story back up in Numbers 27:12-23.

How did the Lord say Moses would die (vv. 12-13)?

What concern did Moses raise (vv. 16-17)?

Whom did the Lord identify as Moses' successor (v. 18)?

What is noteworthy about God's description of Joshua (v. 18)?

What did God tell Moses to do with Joshua (vv. 18-23)?

It's appropriate that the Lord chose Joshua to succeed Moses. He had served under Moses' leadership in humility and with patience. He was a man "in whom is the Spirit" (v. 18). Were you surprised by that description? I was, and I wasn't. There aren't many people in the Old Testament who are described in such a way. Usually, it was a temporary situation. But here, it seems it was a matter of fact. This might explain why he was so able to endure, have patience, and exhibit faith among a people given to fear and complaining.

Look up each of the following passages:

JUDGES 3:7-11

PSALM 51:11

DANIEL 4:8

What similarities do you see in the lives of these Spirit-filled men?

The difference between Moses and Joshua's leadership is how they interacted with the Lord. Moses met with Him face-to-face in the tabernacle, but Joshua had to rely on Eleazar the priest to inquire of the Lord on his behalf. Maybe the forty days and forty nights on the outskirts of the cloud of God and tarrying at the edge of the tent of meeting prepared him. He had always received the word of the Lord from another man, and, it seems, that was enough for Joshua.

STRONG AND COURAGEOUS

In the following verses, underline main words that appear repeatedly:

Joshua the son of Nun, who stands before you, he shall enter. Encourage him, for he shall cause Israel to inherit it.

DEUTERONOMY 1:38

But charge Joshua, and encourage and strengthen him, for he shall go over at the head of this people, and he shall put them in possession of the land that you shall see.

DEUTERONOMY 3:28

Then Moses summoned Joshua and said to him in the sight of all Israel, "Be strong and courageous, for you shall go with this people into the land that the LORD has sworn to their fathers to give them, and you shall put them in possession of it.

DEUTERONOMY 31:7

And the LORD commissioned Joshua the son of Nun and said, "Be strong and courageous, for you shall bring the people of Israel into the land that I swore to give them. I will be with you."

DEUTERONOMY 31:23

Be strong and courageous, for you shall cause this people to inherit the land that I swore to their fathers to give them.

JOSHUA 1:6

Only be strong and very courageous, being careful to do according to all the law that Moses my servant commanded you.

JOSHUA 1:7a

Have I not commanded you? Be strong and courageous. Do not be frightened, and do not be dismayed, for the LORD your God is with you wherever you go.

JOSHUA 1:9

Based on what you've read about Joshua's life, why do you think the Lord reminded him to be "strong and courageous" so often?

What is one area of your own life where you need the Lord's reminder that strength and courage can be found in Him?

It would take strength and courage to succeed in the places where one's mentor had failed. This is no knock on Moses. He had travailed with the people of Israel. He saw and performed miracles and wonders we can only imagine. He is among the saints commended for their faith in Hebrews 11. Moses was not a failure, but he did fail to enter the promised land.

This was no small mantle to receive. Joshua would need to be reminded that it would take strength and courage to lead the people into God's promise.

As you look back over today's lesson, what part stands out to you most? With what do you identify most?

Have you ever been in a situation where you had to be someone's "Joshua"? Are you there now? What challenge or encouragement can you draw from his life?

THE SHEPHERD

When Moses expressed his concern for the people of Israel, he asked the Lord that they would "not be like sheep without a shepherd" (Num. 27:17, NIV). The Lord responded with His choice of a shepherd—Joshua. The Lord provided many "shepherds" to care for His people over their history, but He eventually gave them the best Shepherd—Jesus. Jesus, whose Hebrew name is *Yeshua* (also translated Joshua), fought the battle with sin and death and won.[4]
He leads His people into the land of promise, our eternal inheritance. He is the Good Shepherd who lays down His life for his sheep (John 10:11). There are no chinks in His armor, no deficiency or rebellion in His leadership. We can trust Him to never fail or give up on His sheep.

DAY THREE
A PLEASING AROMA

Pause. Breathe. Pray.

My grandparents lived on a farm just an hour south of downtown Dallas. They raised cattle and grew feed corn, the only crop tough enough to thrive in the "black gumbo" soil. Besides the corn, there were the mesquite trees. Rain was too sparse and the winds too strong to allow many other species of trees to survive. They're not much to look at, but when burned, their aroma is hard to beat.

My grandfather mastered the art of mesquite grilled chicken slathered with barbecue sauce. It was a long process that started midmorning and didn't conclude until the table was set for dinner. The whole day we were all taunted with the mingling of mesquite smoke and sizzling chicken without the satisfaction of taking a bite. But once my grandfather figured they were fall-off-the-bone ready, he always found us eager and hungry with knife and fork in hand.

The distinct scent of mesquite smoke always reminds me of my grandfather and his famous mouth-watering barbecue chicken. Isn't it interesting how certain smells remind us of people or places? They unlock memories that we forgot we had.

As we read Numbers 28–29, notice how often the words "pleasing aroma" occur. I can't help but think that the Lord designed us to connect smells and memories, not just for sentimental reasons, but to remind us of who He is, who we are, and what He has done for us.

Read Numbers 28–29.

This section of Numbers is a calendar of sorts. The offerings required for various occasions are outlined in Numbers 28 and 29 in order of frequency and then by date. We'll survey the feasts and then fill out a table that helps us visualize how many animals were required to fulfill the Lord's requirements.

Record Leviticus 23:1-2 below.

Leviticus 23 outlines seven feasts that the people of Israel were commanded to observe in the promised land. The purpose of the feasts was to provide regular reminders of the character of God and scheduled opportunities for worship and rest.

> **Skim Leviticus 23 for a summary of the feasts. These feasts are repeated in Numbers 28–29. Use the prompts below to record the details of each one.**

THE SABBATH

Before God gave instructions to Moses about the seven feasts, He emphasized the practice of Sabbath.

> **What does Leviticus 23:3 say about the Sabbath?**

FEAST NUMBER ONE: THE PASSOVER

> **According to Leviticus 23:5, when was Passover celebrated?**

> **What is the significance of Passover? (Think or turn back to Session Two!)**

FEAST NUMBER TWO: THE FEAST OF UNLEAVENED BREAD

> **According to Leviticus 23:6, when did the Feast of Unleavened Bread begin?**

> **What were the people supposed to do? For how long?**

> **How does Exodus 12:14-19 elaborate on the observance of this feast?**

FEAST NUMBER THREE: THE FEAST OF FIRSTFRUITS

According to Leviticus 23:9-11, when did this tradition begin?

What did the priest wave before the Lord during this feast (v. 11)?

This feast was an opportunity for God's people to worship Him by giving Him back a portion of the abundant crops He provided for them in the promised land. It was a scheduled reminder that God had been good to the nation of Israel, and her blessings warranted His praise.

FEAST NUMBER FOUR: THE FEAST OF WEEKS

The Feast of Weeks occured seven weeks after Passover (Lev. 23:15-22). It was a celebration at the end of the wheat harvest that commemorated the Lord's provision and sustenance of His people. In Greek, this feast was called Pentecost (meaning fifty days) (Acts 2:1).[5]

FEAST NUMBER FIVE: FEAST OF TRUMPETS

The Feast of Trumpets was a lively day of celebration. Since it occurred on the first day of the month, not only were the Israelites to celebrate the feast, they were also to observe the daily and monthly offerings. Talk about an epic barbecue! This feast marked the beginning of Israel's agricultural year and was proclaimed with a blast of trumpets (Lev. 23:24).

FEAST NUMBER SIX: THE DAY OF ATONEMENT

According to Leviticus 23:27, when was the Day of Atonement observed?

What were the people restricted from doing (Lev. 23:28-30)?

The Day of Atonement was a solemn assembly. In Leviticus 23 the people were commanded to "afflict [them]selves" (vv. 27,32), which is often interpreted to mean they fasted.[6] On this day, the priest would take two male goats and a ram from the people. First, the priest would have to offer the bull to atone for his own sin. Then, one goat was sacrificed before the Lord as an offering to atone for the sin of the people. The priest would lay his hands on the second goat and confess the iniquities, transgressions, and sins of the people over it. (See Lev. 16.) Though all of the feasts point forward to the gospel, this feast in particular was a somber foreshadowing of the coming sacrifice of Christ for the sins of mankind.

FEAST NUMBER SEVEN: FEAST OF BOOTHS

The Feast of Booths was "a seven-day feast that commemorates God's provision for Israel during the wilderness wanderings, and also his present provision for his people."[7] The celebration was full of thanksgiving to God for a bountiful harvest. The "booths" were tents that the people were to construct and dwell in during the feast. This experientially reminded them of the booths, or tents, that the people lived in during the wilderness. The eighth-day festival that immediately followed was separate from the Feast of Booths and was marked by much rejoicing.

What do all these feasts reveal about God and His people?

Has God ever used an experience to remind you of His past faithfulness? Write about that below.

Flip back to Numbers 28–29. In the table below, mark how many bulls, rams, lambs, or goats were required for each occasion. (I promise there's a point to this exercise!) Remember that the daily offerings were just that, required daily.

OCCASION	BURNT OFFERINGS (Bulls | Rams | Lambs)	SIN OFFERING (Goat)
Daily (28:3-8)		
Sabbath (28:9-10)		
Monthly (28:11-15)		
Unleavened Bread (28:17-25)		
Feast of Weeks (28:26-31)		
Feast of Trumpets (29:1-6)		
Day of Atonement (29:7-11)		
Feast of Booths Day One (29:12-16)		
Day Two (29:17-19)		
Day Three (29:20-22)		
Day Four (29:23-25)		
Day Five (29:26-28)		
Day Six (29:29-31)		
Day Seven (29:32-34)		
Day Eight (29:35-38)		

The meat required for these feasts was quite substantial. This means the Lord would make good on His promise to Israel, that the land would provide for her needs abundantly. The aroma coming from the land of Israel, her promised land, must have rivaled my grandfather's mesquite grilled barbecue chicken! After all, we see that these offerings were a "pleasing aroma" to the Lord! While the regular sacrifice of meat probably did smell good, what "smelled" better to the Lord was the people's obedience.

Read the following and make observations:

But thanks be to God, who in Christ always leads us in triumphal procession, and through us spreads the fragrance of the knowledge of him everywhere. For we are the aroma of Christ to God among those who are being saved and among those who are perishing, to one a fragrance from death to death, to the other a fragrance from life to life.

2 CORINTHIANS 2:14-16a

How do you think Israel was a precursor to this "aroma of Christ" (v. 15)?

Picturing the continual offerings in the midst of Israel got my imagination going. I can visualize smoke rising from the burnt offerings on the altar, the scent carried on the breeze to nearby peoples and tribes. To some neighbors, it might be a welcomed smell. They had heard of Israel and her God—the miracles He had done in and through her. Surely, they were curious about this unique nation. Others might have been repulsed by the smell. They'd heard Israel was relentless, dogmatically claiming the land as her inheritance.

To one group, Israel was the fragrance of life. To another, the fragrance of death.

As Christians, we don't offer burnt offerings anymore. We don't carry the literal smell of smoke on our clothes and hair. Jesus is the offering for us. He laid down His life. It's His obedience that rises as a pleasing aroma to the Father. We do, however, carry the aroma of Christ—"the fragrance of the knowledge of him" (v. 14). Our lives are "living sacrifice[s]" (Rom. 12:1) that smell good to those who are looking for and longing for Christ, and they stink a bit to those who want nothing to do with Him. It is possible to repel people for the wrong reasons, though.

What could the wrong reasons be?

Smelling like Jesus means living and loving like He did. When we miss that mark, it means humbly owning up to it, asking forgiveness from others, and embracing the grace afforded to us by Jesus' perfect life and sacrifice. We can't do this on our own. We need the help of the Holy Spirit and to believe the guarantee that we are loved and accepted by God because of the gift of salvation, not because we have achieved it by our works.

Take a brief inventory of your life. How do you smell (spiritually-speaking, of course!)? Is your life a pleasing aroma to Christ and others?

Close in prayer. Ask the Father to show you how to smell more like Christ. Receive the grace He has for you because of the pleasing aroma Christ has offered on your behalf.

VOWS AND VENGEANCE

Pause. Breathe. Pray.

Vows are becoming less and less understood in our day and time. The only places we file the term are in hyper-spiritual cases of cult-like religion or on wedding days. These in the latter file cabinet don't always hold the same weight today as they were originally meant to hold. Our culture sees marriage vows as retractable, not permanent. "'Til death do us part" is often more like, "'Til I don't feel like doing this anymore." Of course, there are reasons for divorce that are biblically protected and simply a part of this fallen world, but, for the most part, Western culture has weakened the meaning of marriage and marriage vows.

In contrast, in the Bible, vows are taken seriously. In Numbers 6 we saw the solemnity that came with keeping the Nazirite vow. Any vow before God or with man was to be considered carefully before making it. We see this again in Numbers 30.

Read Numbers 30. Use the chart below to record who made vows to the Lord and what instructions were recorded for keeping or violating vows.

WHO MADE THE VOW?	SPECIFIC INSTRUCTIONS GIVEN
A man (v. 2)	
A young woman in her father's house (vv. 3-5)	
A young married woman who made a vow before marriage (vv. 6-8)	
A divorced or widowed woman (v. 9)	
A married woman (vv. 10-15)	

While these types of vows may feel foreign to us, the Lord is still serious about the weight of our words. We covered this in Session Two's personal study, but it might be a great opportunity to check how we're doing with our words.

How are you doing with letting your yes be yes and your no be no?

Is there something you have avoided, delayed, or ignored that you know the Lord is nudging you to address? Now, I'm not giving you free reign to "speak your mind" or let someone "have it." I'm talking about something that is the *good you know you ought to do* (see Jas. 4:17) that you haven't done yet.

VENGEANCE ON MIDIAN

It might seem like a strange transition from vows to vengeance, but it's likely the writer of Numbers was making a point. The relationship between God and His people is likened to a father and his children or a husband and his wife numerous times in Scripture. Israel had previously made a vow to devote the cities of Canaan to destruction. (See Num. 21:2.) The very next scene put that vow to the test. Would they fulfill it?

Read Numbers 31.

What was Moses' last task before he was "gathered to [his] people" (v. 2)?

Whom was Israel going to war against? Why?

My husband, Matt, has made it clear that he wants a "good death." I don't bring this topic up often with him. I'd rather talk about a "good life"! But I know what he means by the phrase. He wants to die doing what he loves or fighting for what he believes. He'd rather go out in a blaze of glory or after a long life of faithful, radical obedience than to flicker out in a hospital bed. I don't think he gets much choice in the matter, but I respect his desire.

For Moses, it looked like he was getting what Matt would call a "good death." The Lord gave Moses a heads up that his death was near (v. 2). Basically something like, *Moses, you're going to lead the people to take vengeance on their enemy Midian, and then I'm going to go ahead and bring you home.* Moses got to faithfully fulfill one last mission before being gathered to his people.

The rest of chapter 31 is one of those accounts that is hard to reconcile with who we know the Lord and His people to be. The Lord instructed Israel to execute His vengeance on the Midianites. The men of Israel killed, plundered, and took women and children captive. This sounds far from laying one's life down for a friend or valuing others over one's self. So how does this all fit together?

In Ephesians 6 the apostle Paul revealed that our true enemies are not other people, but "the rulers . . . the authorities . . . the cosmic powers over this present darkness" (v. 12). In other words, our enemy is Satan and the entities and cosmic power structures he has established. He is the thief who "comes only to steal and kill and destroy" (John 10:10). Ultimately, he will be overthrown completely at Christ's return. Until then, we are to suit up like the fighting men of Israel. But instead of using man-made armor, we are to put on the whole armor of God.

Turn to Ephesians 6:14-18 to help you fill in the blanks below.

- The belt of _____;

- The breastplate of _____;

- As shoes for your feet . . . the readiness given by the gospel of _____;

- The shield of _____;

- The helmet of _____;

- The sword of the _____, which is the _____ _____ _____.

How many of the items are used as protection? How many are used for proactive fighting?

This might seem like a major rabbit trail, but I need you to stay with me for a minute. (I promise it will eventually make sense!) Our friends hired a crew of men to clear out some trees and brush on their property. I watched them roll in with all their tools, saws, and other implements and thought, *OK, here we go! The fun is about to begin!* To my surprise, though, they took over an hour just preparing for their work. They put on their boots and long-sleeved shirts, doused their entire wardrobe with bug repellant, sharpened their saws, filled tanks with gas, and checked oil levels. The work could not begin until they were completely prepared. Like the tree clearing crew, we are to take care in putting on the whole armor before we start wielding our swords in the struggle against our enemy.

But we must wield the sword, the Word of God. We must fight the lies of the enemy with the truth of God. We must believe that God is good, that He wants good for His children, and that a life fully surrendered to following Him is the most satisfying and fulfilling life we can imagine.

In what ways do you see believers actively using the armor of God today?

How have you "Put on the whole armor of God" in your own life (v. 11)?

The spoils of Israel's battle against Midian were substantial—sheep, cattle, donkeys, gold, and jewelry. Half of the livestock went to the men who fought and the other half to those who stayed behind. Of both groups, a percentage was given to the priests and Levites. The soldiers gave one out of five hundred (Num. 31:28), and the people gave one out of fifty (v. 30). We see the Lord honor those who had been willing to give their lives for Israel by requiring an offering that was at a significantly lower percentage than the congregation's.

According to Exodus 30, if the Israelites took a census, they were to "give a ransom for [each] life to the LORD" (v. 12). This explains the exchange at the end of Numbers 31. It appears the officers of Israel's army took a census to see if they had lost any men in battle. Astonishingly, they hadn't lost one. In order to follow the Lord's instructions in taking a census and to avoid provoking a plague, the officers brought articles of gold as their ransom. However, they brought more than was required.

Why do you think they gave so generously?

It's easy to imagine the officers were abundantly grateful for God's protection and provision and wanted to respond accordingly. Moses and Eleazar received their contributions and placed them in "the tent of meeting, as a memorial for the people of Israel before the LORD" (v. 54).

Why was it important for the people to have a visual reminder of their victory?

A WOMAN, A VOW, AND A CONTRIBUTION

Hannah's story, which took place years after Israel would settle in the promised land, is a lovely reflection of the precepts of Numbers 30–31. Hannah was married to a man named Elkanah. She desperately wanted children but could not conceive. On one trip with her husband to the house of the Lord, Hannah found herself pouring out her heart before God within earshot of Eli the priest. Her prayer was so emotional, Eli accused her of being drunk. She humbly clarified her situation. She wasn't drunk; she was desperate for a child. She made a vow to the Lord.

Record Hannah's vow found in 1 Samuel 1:11.

When Hannah bore a son, she named him Samuel, meaning, "I have asked for him from the LORD" (v. 20). When Samuel was weaned, she took him to Eli and "lent him to the LORD" (v. 28) for the rest of his days. That child became the priest who would anoint the first King of Israel, Saul, and his successor, King David. It's apparent Elkanah approved of Hannah's vow since she fulfilled it. The extravagance of her gratitude is verbalized in her beautiful prayer. Hannah's prayer, or song, in response to the Lord honoring her vow, reminds us that the Lord is truly God and well able to conquer our enemies. We don't have to fight in our own strength or take vengeance into our own hands. We can rest knowing, "There is none holy like the LORD . . . there is no rock like our God" (1 Sam. 2:2). Let's read it together.

My heart exults in the LORD;
    my horn is exalted in the LORD.
My mouth derides my enemies,
    because I rejoice in your salvation.
There is none holy like the LORD:
    for there is none besides you;
    there is no rock like our God.
Talk no more so very proudly,
    let not arrogance come from your mouth;
for the LORD is a God of knowledge,
    and by him actions are weighed.
The bows of the mighty are broken,
    but the feeble bind on strength.
Those who were full have hired themselves out for bread,
    but those who were hungry have ceased to hunger.
The barren has borne seven,
    but she who has many children is forlorn.
The LORD kills and brings to life;
    he brings down to Sheol and raises up.
The LORD makes poor and makes rich;
    he brings low and he exalts.
He raises up the poor from the dust;
    he lifts the needy from the ash heap
to make them sit with princes
    and inherit a seat of honor.
For the pillars of the earth are the LORD's,
    and on them he has set the world.
He will guard the feet of his faithful ones,
    but the wicked shall be cut off in darkness,
    for not by might shall a man prevail.
The adversaries of the LORD shall be broken to pieces;
    against them he will thunder in heaven.
The LORD will judge the ends of the earth;
    he will give strength to his king
    and exalt the horn of his anointed.

1 SAMUEL 2:1b-10

DAY FIVE
INTENTIONS

Pause. Breathe. Pray.

Yesterday, we closed with Hannah's faithfulness to keep her vow to the Lord. Today, we will see another group of people promise to keep theirs. The parallel of their stories is notable. There's a desire, a request, a misunderstanding, and a promise. Hannah desired a child. She asked the Lord to fulfill her request. Eli the priest mistakenly believed she was drunk. Hannah clarified and revealed her vow to Eli. The Lord granted her request, and she kept her word.

Read Numbers 32.

Why was the land of Jazer and Gilead attractive to the people of Reuben and Gad (v. 1)?

To whom did they submit their request (vv. 2-5)?

Summarize Moses' response (vv. 6-15).

Whom did Moses think they were acting like (v. 14)?

What did the people of Reuben and Gad offer to do (vv. 16-18)?

Summarize Moses' response (vv. 20-24).

What "if, then" promise did Moses hold them to?

What would happen if the people of Reuben and Gad didn't keep their end of the deal?

Write Numbers 32:23 below.

Starting in verse 28, whom did Moses inform about the promise the people of Reuben and Gad made? Why do you think he did this?

THE DESIRE AND REQUEST

The people of Reuben and Gad surveyed the hill country on the eastern border of the promised land and saw that it was perfect for raising cattle. They were the original ranchers. I wonder if they thought it just couldn't get any better than that spot. What did they know of the promised land? Only the stories whispered by their parents—giants, land that devours, and trouble. Did that play into their decision? We can't tell. The narrator doesn't let us see into their hearts and minds. He withholds judgment and instead lets us peek into Moses' interpretation of their request.

THE MISUNDERSTANDING

Have you ever asked a spouse or friend a loaded question, but you didn't know it was loaded until you got their response? Just me? The Reubenites and Gadites might have anticipated Moses' severe reaction, but perhaps they didn't. They hadn't known Egypt. They were children of the wilderness. It's all they knew. Moses knew the oppression in Egypt. He knew the murmuring and rebellion of the wilderness. He knew what it was like to see an entire nation walk right up to the promised land and forfeit entrance. He was not going to let that happen again. What might have seemed a simple request to the people of Reuben and Gad was tiptoeing toward apostasy in Moses' mind.

He assumed he knew the people's intentions: to follow in the footsteps of their parents by refusing to enter the promised land and thus leading the rest of the people astray.

Think back on what you've learned. List any past incidents that come to mind that might lead Moses to respond in this way.

THE PROMISE

The people, it seems, were not offended by Moses' stern response. Instead, they offered a solution and proof that they would not forsake their brothers. If Moses would let them build sheepfolds (stonewalls that were the predecessor of barbed wire and fence posts) for their livestock and cities for the women and children, they would join the other tribes in taking the promised land. Not only did they promise to go with the people, they offered to be the front line. They weren't afraid of the promised land. It wasn't fear that kept them in Gilead. It was opportunity. In the end, their settling of Jazer and Gilead expanded Israel's territory.

Although Moses was not fully convinced, he moved forward with the agreement. He made the arrangement known to Eleazar, Joshua, and the heads of the tribes. The Lord had shown him that he would not enter with them, so he needed to make sure the leaders knew. They would be responsible for holding the tribes of Reuben and Gad to their word.

What does this interaction reveal about the hearts of these men? How is it different from what we saw in their parents?

A WARNING

The warning Moses gave the Reubenites and Gadites is a truth that stands the test of time: your sin will find you out. We see this evidenced in the headlines, in the poorly-recorded sound bites and grainy videos of high-profile people in less-than-savory situations. Or when our carefully crafted alibis stop adding up. Even if we carry a secret to the grave, the Lord already knows. You can't hide from Him.

And do not fear those who kill the body but cannot kill the soul. Rather fear him who can destroy both soul and body in hell.

MATTHEW 10:28

When you read Moses' warning, did you feel a pit in your stomach? Is there sin in your life that you've vowed to carry to the grave?

Israel's story in the Book of Numbers is a cautionary tale. It's a warning of what happens when God's people give in to fear instead of trusting God in faith. That's why I've given you multiple chances to divulge hidden sin in this study. Sin is not your friend. It will not stay quiet. It will give you away.

Is there still a hidden sin in your life? Take a moment now to pray, asking for forgiveness from the God who sees even our hidden sins.

THE MORAL OF THE STORY

So what do we do with the account of Gad, Reuben, and the half-tribe of Manasseh (who joined the other two tribes in Gilead)? First, it's a part of the whole story of Scripture and is worth knowing on its own. Second, the interaction between Moses and the tribes sounds all too familiar. I have been on both sides of this situation.

I have been like Moses, somewhat offended by and suspicious of someone's request. A past experience or fear colored my perspective. It made me question their motives. Were they pure or impure? Manipulative or earnest? This passage reminds me that I cannot rightly measure the intentions of others. I can't truly decipher my own, so how can I determine another's?

I have been in the people's shoes as well. I have asked a question or made a request that evoked a strong reaction. I probably responded with indignation. How dare they assume my motives were ill-intentioned? The answer? Past experience!

How about you? Have you found yourself in either situation? How did it turn out?

The results have been mixed when I've been met with these circumstances. Sometimes my fears were proven unfounded, and, sadly, other times, they turned out true. Either way, the Lord has used both kinds of encounters to mature me. I've seen that I can't make assumptions, but I've also realized I can be cautious without growing bitter.

Take a minute to examine your heart. Has bitterness grown in places you've been hurt or led astray by ill-intentioned people? Are you willing to hand that to the Lord and forgive others even if they haven't explicitly asked for forgiveness?

The beauty of life in Christ is that we get to start over with Him day after day, minute after minute. We get to release to Him those who've hurt or used us. We don't have to supervise them. The Lord knows. Remember, if there's sin on their part, it will find them out.

The Reubenites and Gadites were wise to offer a solution, and Moses was shrewd to hold them to it. The compromise gave Moses a plan to fall back on and the people a chance to prove themselves. Win-win.

Did the men of Reuben, Gad, and half of Manasseh keep their word? Turn to Joshua 4:12-13 and record what you find.

Close in a prayer of surrender and release.

Lord, I surrender any right I feel like I have to judge or supervise someone else's intentions. Only You know the true state of his/her heart and mine. Cleanse me from sin. Forgive me for trying to do Your job. Help me to trust You with my intentions and others'. I release anyone who has hurt or used me, knowing that You are the perfect Judge. Thank You for the forgiveness I have received in Christ. Help me to extend that to others. Amen.

I've provided some discussion questions here to get the conversation started. Feel free to discuss what you learned throughout the week of study, ask any questions you may have, and share what God is teaching you.

DISCUSSION QUESTIONS

Are you tempted to believe that you can sin in isolation—that your sin doesn't affect the people around you? If you considered the impact your sin has on others in your life and even generations that will come after you, how much does it change the way you live?

If you had to pick one—are you more apt to rebel against God or live in fear? Can you unpack why?

Does it relieve you to know that God asks you to be faithful and not perfect (because Christ was perfect for us)? How might that freedom to not be perfect cause you to love God and love others?

What sort of residue do you want to leave for the next generation?

Teaching sessions available for purchase or rent at *LifeWay.com/WithUsInTheWilderness*

THERE'S NO PLACE LIKE HOME

These are the commandments and the rules
that the LORD commanded through Moses
to the people of Israel in the plains of
Moab by the Jordan at Jericho.

NUMBERS 36:13

DAY ONE
LOOKING BACK

Pause. Breathe. Pray.

We have almost made it through the entire Book of Numbers. Can you believe it? The book that makes others fall off the Bible-in-a-year-reading wagon has now become a favorite, right? I am so proud of you! Let's keep going!

Read Numbers 33:1-49.

Read 2 Timothy 3:16-17 and Revelation 21:5.

In light of those verses and what you've read so far in this study, why do you think God commanded Moses to write down all these details?

List the locations that sound familiar in Numbers 33. Make note of events that happened at those sites.

List the locations that don't sound familiar.

Hopefully your hand didn't cramp too much. My goal was not to bring back memories of handwriting practice, but to jog your memory concerning the places we've "been" and make note of the places we haven't. Every location name was known to the people and to God. Children were born there; loved ones lost there; failures, successes, epiphanies, disappointments, quarrels, and reconciliation made there.

These place names meant something.

Today's primary exercise won't look like much on paper, but it will take some time for quiet reflection.

As Moses made an account of all the places Israel had been on her way out of Egypt and up to the edge of Canaan, I want you to make an account of your own. On the next page, starting with your birthdate, write down any significant events in your life along the timeline. Once you write them down, use the space underneath to detail how the Lord was with you there.

Even if these events happened before you came to Christ, God is omnipresent. There is nowhere He is not. Ask Him to help you see how He was there. Even in the painful moments, ask Him to show you. Remember that He is gracious, compassionate, slow to anger, and abounding in steadfast love (Ps. 103:8; 145:8).

QUESTIONS TO CONSIDER

Did you sense His presence in a new or unique way?

Did He answer a specific prayer?

Did He deal with a particular sin in your life?

Did He provide comfort through His Spirit and His church?

Did He show you something about His character through His Word?

TIMELINE OF MY LIFE

MY BIRTHDAY

As you look over the timeline of your life, does your answer about why God would ask Moses to make the list in Numbers 33 change (p. 190)? How so?

We see that Moses took meticulous notes for a record of remembrance. God wants His people to know and remember He is faithful and present. He also wants us to share with others, including future generations, how He has been faithful in our own lives.

Once you've finished the exercise, lay your hands on the pages (there's nothing magical about it, just symbolic) and pray. Thank the Lord for being with you through it all. Ask Him to help you see Him as compassionate and tender in the hard moments. Receive the forgiveness readily available to you because of Christ over the moments that bring shame. Dedicate the timeline yet to be completed to His care.

DAY TWO
BOUNDARIES

Pause. Breathe. Pray.

The word *boundary* can be a polarizing term. We like boundaries when we're the ones making them. After all, "good fences make good neighbors." Here's what's "mine," and there's what's "yours." However, we don't like boundaries when someone else imposes them on us. This starts early in life. In preschool rooms and playrooms, we hear this work out between toddlers. One child declares a toy is "mine," but another begs to differ, and then chaos ensues.

Boundaries are good. They keep us safe. They help us know what's ours to take care of and what's not. At the end of Numbers 33 and the beginning of 34, we see the Lord set boundaries on the people's worship and the land they are to inherit.

BOUNDARIES OF WORSHIP

Read Numbers 33:50-56.

List what they are to drive out, destroy, and take.

DRIVE OUT	DESTROY	TAKE

How were the Israelites told to apportion the land (v. 54)?

What was the warning if they didn't drive out the Canaanites (vv. 55-56)?

Numbers 33:56 and Deuteronomy 28:63 provide parallel warnings from God if the Israelites failed to drive out the inhabitants of the land. Summarize the Lord's warning.

This section of Numbers 33 is a legal matter: The Lord gave commandments to Israel that they were to keep or else suffer the consequences. He set a boundary with them in their worship by commanding that they drive out the inhabitants, destroy their idols, and take and settle the land. To leave the people and their idols would make them susceptible to forsaking worship of the one true God. Spoiler alert: despite many warnings and exhortations to keep this commandment, Israel had a hard time following through. The idols and gods of Canaan were stumbling blocks that tripped the Israelites up on the path of obedience. They were barbs in their eyes that made truth and the Lord hard to see clearly. As thorns in their sides, they caused unnecessary pain and suffering. Eventually, after generations of continued rebellion, many in Israel lost the land and were sent into exile.

Despite Israel's faithlessness, the Lord continued to be faithful. He always gave the people a chance to repent, turn away from their idols, and come back to Him. At just the right time, He sent His Son, Jesus, who is the better Moses, the better Joshua, the better Israel. He never grumbled. He never rebelled. He was obedient to the point of death. Through His obedience, we get an inheritance that can never be lost (1 Pet. 1:4). One day, He will return and make all things new.

The propensity for God's people to be tempted by other gods hasn't changed. Our idols might not be made of stone or metal, but they still hold power over us. I've started a list of familiar current-day idols.

Add any other idols that come to mind in the remaining blanks.

- What other people think
- Wealth
- Status
- Friendships
- Being a part of "the in-crowd"
- Substances

- Our children
- "Perfection"
- _____
- _____
- _____
- _____

I appreciate Dr. Timothy Keller's definition in his book, *Counterfeit Gods*:

> What is an idol? It is anything more important to you than God, anything that absorbs your heart and imagination more than God, anything you seek to give you what only God can give.
>
> An idol is whatever you look at and say, in your heart of hearts, "If I have that, then I'll feel my life has meaning, then I'll know I have value, then I'll feel significant and secure." There are many ways to describe that kind of relationship to something, but perhaps the best one is *worship*.[1]

Turn to Colossians 3:5-10 and answer the following:

What does Colossians 3:5 list as "idolatry"?

What are we to do with idolatry?

How is this similar to the commandment God gave Israel concerning the inhabitants of the promised land?

Look at the list of idols on the previous page. Star the ones that tempt you most.

How might these idols become a stumbling block, barb in your eye, or thorn in your side?

Now, look at Dr. Keller's definition of an *idol*. Is there something or someone in your life that fits that description?

The first step in forsaking idols is recognizing and naming them. Hopefully, you were able to identify at least one. If you're idol-free, praise God! I've found there are seasons where the struggle is more "real" than others—times when I've had to keep "tearing down the high places" in my heart. There are also seasons where the idols aren't as alluring. I can usually trace that to two different roots: suffering that keeps me clinging to the only true Anchor of my soul or an intense awareness of God's unequaled beauty and love. Thank God for His kindness in that!

The next step is bringing those idols to God and "telling on them" out loud. It could look like:

> *Father, I have given my heart and worship to _____ for far too long. Forgive me for forsaking You for this idol. You alone deserve my worship. I renounce the lie that _____ is better than You. I give You all my worship. Thank You for Your forgiveness and the gift of grace to walk in obedience. Help me, Holy Spirit, to continue to put away idolatry and put on the things that look like You (Col. 3:12-14). Amen.*

BOUNDARIES OF THE LAND

Read Numbers 34.

Turn to the map on page 224 and outline the border of the promised land with your favorite color pen or marker (or whatever you have available!). Use a different color for the border of Gilead.

Who was in charge of dividing the land (vv. 17-18)? Why do you think God chose these men to be in charge of dividing the land?

In the table below, list the tribal chiefs along with their tribe.

LIST OF TRIBAL CHIEFS	TRIBAL CHIEF TRIBE

Things are getting real. The Lord has named the men from each tribe who are to represent their people in the division of the land. He is proving that not only will they enter the land, they will be able to take it.

The size of their land is not exorbitant. The boundaries fit their needs. The Lord could have given them the entire earth, but for some reason and at this time, He chose this portion and no more.

As we survey the boundaries of Israel's promised land, I am reminded of a psalm of David.

> Preserve me, O God, for in you I take refuge.
> I say to the LORD, "You are my Lord;
>   I have no good apart from you."
> As for the saints in the land, they are the excellent ones,
>   in whom is all my delight.
> The sorrows of those who run after another god shall multiply;
>   their drink offerings of blood I will not pour out
>   or take their names on my lips.
> The LORD is my chosen portion and my cup;
>   you hold my lot.
> The lines have fallen for me in pleasant places;
>   indeed, I have a beautiful inheritance.
> I bless the LORD who gives me counsel;
>   in the night also my heart instructs me.
> I have set the LORD always before me;
>   because he is at my right hand, I shall not be shaken.
> Therefore my heart is glad, and my whole being rejoices;
>   my flesh also dwells secure.
> For you will not abandon my soul to Sheol,
>   or let your holy one see corruption.
> You make known to me the path of life;
>   in your presence there is fullness of joy;
>   at your right hand are pleasures forevermore.

PSALM 16

Underline the parts of the psalm that echo the themes in the Book of Numbers. In particular, notice the following:

- Land
- Forsaking other gods
- Portion
- Lot

- Inheritance
- Dwelling
- Path

The hope and struggle of humans hasn't changed over thousands of years. We all hope for a place to call home where we're loved and accepted, where we find value and meaning. Essentially, we all long for the promised land—the kingdom of God. But we struggle with the boundaries God puts around it. Boundaries that show us what is acceptable worship and what is not. We want the kingdom without the King. We want it on our terms. However, it's impossible to have it that way. The heart of the promised land is the King. The point of it all is God making His dwelling with us. He is our portion. He is our beautiful inheritance. He alone holds pleasures forevermore.

DAY THREE
CITIES

Pause. Breathe. Pray.

If you were to look at my social media pages, especially Instagram®, you would see a common theme: I love nature. Pastures full of wildflowers, the rolling Texas Hill Country, majestic oak trees, and stunning sunsets fill my feed. While I make my home in the suburbs, I am a country girl at heart. A dear friend of mine is the complete opposite. Give her all the concrete, hustle and bustle, and graffiti of the city. I'll be honest, I love the idea of living in the country, but I'm sure the moment I run out of toilet paper or need a last minute item from the grocery store thirty minutes away, I'll be questioning my devotion.

After forty years in the wilderness, I can imagine the Israelites were eager to finally settle in cities, build homes, and cultivate the land. To them, the city meant security and stability. So it's no surprise to see the Lord give instructions regarding the cities they were to inhabit.

CITIES FOR THE LEVITES

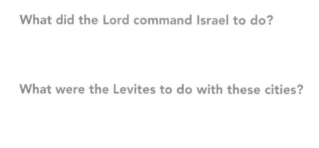

Read Numbers 35:1-8.

What did the Lord command Israel to do?

What were the Levites to do with these cities?

How many cities were they to give the Levites?

How many were cities of refuge?

Who fled to the cities of refuge?

It's fitting that the cities apportioned to the Levites would come after the allotment of land to the other tribes. Like the census, the Levites were separated from the people but also for the people. They were not to serve in the military but in the tabernacle. They were dependent upon the people's generosity while the people were dependent upon their service to the Lord on their behalf.

As we've already covered in the previous sessions, everyone has a part to play. This is still true today. My husband, Matt, and I have served the people of The Village Church for seventeen years now. Vocational ministry definitely has its perks, but it also comes with a fair share (or more) of hardship and heartache. Our livelihood almost completely depends on the generosity of the people of God. We are so grateful for their willingness to give.

Every Christian has a portion in the kingdom of God. Our callings may be different, but we are all commanded to use what God has given us—our talents, our opportunities, our resources—to build His kingdom.

CITIES OF REFUGE

Read Numbers 35:9-34.

What is the difference between a manslayer and a murderer?

How long would the manslayer live in the city of refuge?

How many witnesses were required to convict a person of murder?

According to verses 33-34, why was the Lord serious about handling murder or manslaughter in this way?

Why do you think whole cities were dedicated as refuge for manslayers?

The author of Numbers further explains the purpose of the cities of refuge. They were for the protection of manslayers before they were judged and once they were convicted of unintentional murder. The avenger of blood was the kinsman-redeemer given the duty to avenge his relative's death. If the manslayer was convicted of intentional murder, the avenger of blood would complete his duty by killing the offender. If it was determined that the manslayer killed the person unintentionally, he would live in the city of refuge until the high priest died. Either way, the satisfaction for the crime was death. For the murderer, his own death. For the manslayer, the high priest's death. Blood for blood.

Isn't it interesting that what made a people and their land unclean before the Lord was the same medium that made them clean? The blood spilled by man whether intentional or not could only be atoned for by blood spilled by the high priest on the altar of God.

How kind is the Lord to provide refuge for those who killed someone accidentally? I can imagine being in a different city provided relief for both the manslayer and the family who lost the loved one. As the manslayer, it would be hard to see the faces of those who loved the person you killed. As the family, it would be equally difficult to see the person who killed your loved one going about life as usual. The Lord knew both needed the change of scenery. Surely that made healing a little easier.

The crown of God's creation is humanity. Only men and women were made in His image. To destroy His image is to seek to destroy Him. This is why murder is no small thing to Him, even if it's unintentional. Jesus expounded on the full extent of murder: it doesn't just happen physically; it first takes place in our hearts.

Turn to Matthew 5:21-24.

What did Jesus liken to murder?

What did Jesus tell us to do if we remember someone has something against us?

Does this hit a little too close to home? Murder is more manageable for my conscience when it can only occur on the outside of my body, but as a matter of the heart, I am guilty as charged. You too? Praise God for His conviction and Jesus' atoning work on our behalf. Because of God's great grace, we can humbly admit our wrong and make things right with our brother or sister who has something against us.

I'm not advocating going to someone who has no idea we have anger in our hearts toward him/her and saying something like, "Hey, I'm sorry for hating your guts. Will you forgive me?" However, I am suggesting that if someone was brought to mind as you read Matthew 5, pray for him/her and for your heart toward him/her. If you know he/she has something against you, humbly ask to meet with him/her to make it right. If not, ask the Lord to change your heart toward him/her and do what you can to put away the anger. I have found praying for that person earnestly helps tremendously.

If this struck a chord with you, start the process of turning from your anger by writing a prayer for yourself and that person here.

DAY FOUR
HEIRESSES AND INHERITANCE

Pause. Breathe. Pray.

For a book with so much emphasis on men, it's interesting to see it wrap up with the obedience of women. While the censuses are dominated by men's names (because men were the ones who would serve in the military and in the tabernacle), we must note that God's promise to Abraham to have offspring like the number of stars cannot happen without women.

HEIRESSES

Read Numbers 36.

What problem do "the heads of the fathers' houses of the clan of the people of Gilead" (v. 1) bring to Moses and the chiefs?

(Side note: how good does it feel to read these verses and actually know what they're talking about? Scripture doesn't have to be cryptic. Isn't that great?)

What was the deal made with the daughters of Zelophehad?

What solution did Moses offer?

When a woman married, any inheritance would become a part of her husband's inheritance. This caused a problem for the daughters of Zelophehad. The whole point of the request they brought to Moses in Numbers 27 was to keep his name with his clan. Marriage to a man of another tribe would undo the arrangement. The Lord provided that the daughters could marry whomever they wanted as long as it was from among the clan of the tribe of their father.

The heart of this provision was to make sure the inheritance was not transferred—that what was promised to Zelophehad would be fulfilled. While he died of (most likely) natural causes in the wilderness, his children were able to inherit their portion of the promised land. The Lord stayed true to His word and the daughters of Zelophehad stayed true to theirs. They married their cousins, the sons of their uncles. This might sound improper (or downright gross), but this was a common and acceptable practice in ancient times.

The inheritance the people of Israel longed for was a land to call their own where God would dwell among them. This started in Eden—the garden where the Lord walked with Adam and Eve in the cool of the day. (See Gen. 3.) It will end when God will remake the heavens and the earth and make His dwelling with man. (See Rev. 21.) All along, God has desired to be with His people, hence, the laws, the regulations, the sacrifices, and the offerings.

OUR INHERITANCE

In 1 Peter 1 the apostle Peter, who was a close friend and disciple of Jesus, wrote a letter to Christians dispersed throughout Asia Minor. His intent was to encourage the believers to remain faithful through suffering and persecution. Their trials were not for nothing. The Lord was using hardship to refine and test them. Not only that, He had prepared an inheritance for them that could not be tainted. Sound familiar?

Read 1 Peter 1:3-9 below. Make notes if you wish!

Blessed be the God and Father of our Lord Jesus Christ! According to his great mercy, he has caused us to be born again to a living hope through the resurrection of Jesus Christ from the dead, to an inheritance that is imperishable, undefiled, and unfading, kept in heaven for you, who by God's power are being guarded through faith for a salvation ready to be revealed in the last time. In this you rejoice, though now for a little while, if necessary, you have been grieved by various trials, so that the tested genuineness of your faith—more precious than gold that perishes though it is tested by fire—may be found to result in praise and glory and honor at the revelation of Jesus Christ. Though you have not seen him, you love him. Though you do not now see him, you believe in him and rejoice with joy that is inexpressible and filled with glory, obtaining the outcome of your faith, the salvation of your souls.

The Israelites had been through their share of trials. The wilderness was the furnace in which they were tested. Some proved faithful. Others did not. The Lord remained faithful throughout.

Our inheritance is not a physical piece of land flowing with milk and honey in the Middle East. It's better than that. It can't wear out from use or famine. It can't be taken from us by hostile forces. It is kept in heaven for us.

> What exactly does it look like though? As Christians, our inheritance involves three things:
>
> • a new body (1 Cor. 15:35-49);
>
> • new heavens and a new earth (2 Pet. 3:13);
>
> • unfettered access to the presence and power of God (Rev. 22:3-5).
>
> Of the three, which are you most looking forward to?

Turning forty this year has reminded me that I am not who I once was. Physical exertion that used to result in a day or so of soreness is taking a greater toll on my body now! True story: I started using a heart monitor for workouts and runs just to see how hard my heart is working (and to earn points at my gym). There are different zones: blue (the lowest rate), green, yellow, and red (the highest rate). My runs were consistently in the red zone, so I immediately made an appointment with my doctor. I thought for sure something was wrong with my heart and I was on the verge of a mild heart attack. The good news is that I am perfectly fine. The bad news is that I'm just out of shape. While I am looking forward to a new "spiritual" body that doesn't grow old, wear out, or get out of shape, I am most looking forward to the unfettered access to the presence of God.

Every human heart was made for intimate fellowship with the Living God. We may fill that longing with every kind of substitute—from relationships with other people, to food, status, or possessions. But only one thing will do: God Himself. For those of us who are Christians, the Spirit dwells in us. He is as close as our own breath. But won't it be amazing to actually see Him, feel Him, and know Him as we are fully known (1 Cor. 13:12)? I have had moments with the Lord when He has felt especially near: in rooms with others crying out to Him, praying, and singing together, but also in the quiet of my own home, all by myself. Those spaces are the foretaste of the unfettered fellowship with the Lover of our souls. On that day, we will have no distraction, only perfect adoration. That's what I'm longing for most.

> **Have you had any "foretaste of the unfettered fellowship" moments? If so, would you be willing to share? If you haven't, would you be willing to ask for it? He loves to give His children good gifts!**

I want to close today with a meditation on Psalm 84. You might be surprised to know who the authors were: the sons of Korah. What a beautiful reminder that the sin of our fathers (and mothers) does not have to be our destiny too. By grace through faith in Jesus Christ, we get to sing a new song. A song of longing for our inheritance—the presence and power of the one true God.

> **If possible, read the psalm on the next page aloud a few times. Make the sons of Korah's prayer your own.**

How lovely is your dwelling place,
    O Lord of hosts!
My soul longs, yes, faints
    for the courts of the Lord;
my heart and flesh sing for joy
    to the living God.
Even the sparrow finds a home,
    and the swallow a nest for herself,
    where she may lay her young,
at your altars, O Lord of hosts,
    my King and my God.
Blessed are those who dwell in your house,
    ever singing your praise! Selah
Blessed are those whose strength is in you,
    in whose heart are the highways to Zion.
As they go through the Valley of Baca
    they make it a place of springs;
    the early rain also covers it with pools.
They go from strength to strength;
    each one appears before God in Zion.
O Lord God of hosts, hear my prayer;
    give ear, O God of Jacob! Selah
Behold our shield, O God;
    look on the face of your anointed!
For a day in your courts is better
    than a thousand elsewhere.
I would rather be a doorkeeper in the house of my God
    than dwell in the tents of wickedness.
For the Lord God is a sun and shield;
    the Lord bestows favor and honor.
No good thing does he withhold
    from those who walk uprightly.
O Lord of hosts,
    blessed is the one who trusts in you!

PSALM 84

MOUNTAINS, WILDERNESS, AND THE PLAINS

Pause. Breathe. Pray.

Just last week, my fourteen-year-old son (our only son) asked to go on a hike with me. We were in the Rocky Mountains on a perfectly clear day with an experienced guide (and did I mention my fourteen-year-old asked me to go?). How could I say no?

If you've ever hiked in higher altitudes, you know the huffing and puffing and absurd heart-pounding that accompanies the climb. What looks like an easy slope toward the rocky summit becomes a serious workout. We took several breaks on the hike to catch our breath and to make sure we were still on the right path. Storms, recent and past, had knocked down familiar landmarks and trees with signs that marked the trail. We made our way slowly but surely, backtracking a few times and carefully climbing over granite domes and through rocky crevices.

After an hour and a half of hiking, we finally reached the top. Words fail to express the beauty of our view. Pike National Forest stretched out before us on all sides—layers of gray and red boulders, lush green valleys, golden hillsides, deep purple mountains in the distance set against the bright blue sky. Pikes Peak rose strong and sure to the south, its summit powdered with snow from the showers the night before. The view from the heights made the hard work of the hike worth it.

I hope you are feeling somewhat of the same satisfaction. We have braved the Book of Numbers together, stumbling through names, numbers, instructions for worship, feasts, murmuring, complaining, earth-swallowing, dust-water-drinking, vows, vengeance, curses-turned-blessings, rebellion, and redemption. We found in Israel's journey our own stories and experiences in the wilderness and, hopefully, the continued promise and presence of God.

Think back over our weeks together. What moments or memories stand out to you?

As we look back on the Book of Numbers and Israel's journey through the wilderness, we can see a pattern established between mountains and wildernesses/plains.

Turn to the texts below and record the landmark mentioned there.

SCRIPTURE	LANDMARK
Leviticus 27:34	Mount _____
Numbers 10:11-12	Wilderness of _____ and Wilderness of _____
Numbers 20:1	Wilderness of ____
Numbers 20:22	Mount _____
Numbers 22:1	Plains of _____
Deuteronomy 34:1	Mount _____

Life seems to be a series of mountaintop moments, wilderness wanderings, and mundane days in the plains. The mountaintop gives us perspective, proximity, and marks transition. Moses met with God on Mount Sinai and received the Law. The priesthood passed from Aaron to Eleazar on Mount Hor. Moses peered into the promised land and left this earthly life on Mount Nebo. On the mountain, we can see life spread out before us. God's rule and reign are evident. His presence is tangible, and our calling seems clear. The experience marks us in a way that we are never the same.

Have you had a mountaintop experience? What did it look like for you? Feel free to include more than one!

In Deuteronomy 8:2-3 Moses explained God's intention for His people's time in the wilderness.

And you shall remember the whole way that the LORD your God has led you these forty years in the wilderness, that he might humble you, testing you to know what was in your heart, whether you would keep his commandments or not. And he humbled you and let you hunger and fed you with manna, which you did not know, nor did your fathers know, that he might make you know that man does not live by bread alone, but man lives by every word that comes from the mouth of the LORD **(emphasis mine).**

The wilderness isn't a mistake or cruel joke. It is a time of testing, not just of our hearts, but our idols—the things we are putting our hope in that are not God. Will they hold up to the fire? Will they deliver us from peril? Will they live up to their promises? Or will they leave us disappointed, or worse yet, dead?

For those currently in a wilderness season, I want to encourage you with this: Very often, the wilderness precedes a season of breakthrough and fruitfulness. The Lord called Moses to lead His people out of Egypt when Moses was keeping his father-in-law's flock in the wilderness (Ex. 3). The people of Israel wandered the wilderness before they came into the promised land. King David fled Saul's wrath in the wilderness (1 Sam.) before taking the throne. John the Baptist was in the wilderness when "the word of God came to [him]" (Luke 3:2), and he began preaching about repentance and preparing the way for the Messiah. Even Jesus was led into the wilderness by the Spirit for forty days before the advent of his public ministry (Luke 4).

The wilderness might seem barren and confusing, but it isn't pointless. The Lord might just be preparing you for a new season. I've seen the Lord use the specific heartache and hardship of the wilderness in my life to serve the season of breakthrough and fruitfulness that followed it. If you are in a wilderness of the soul right now, I am praying that the Lord would refine and humble you. That you would find Him to be faithful and personal. He has not left, nor will He ever leave you. He is with you. This is only a season and will bear fruit in your life and others' lives sooner than you can imagine.

Are you in the wilderness? Will you receive my prayer for you?

Do you know someone who's in the wilderness? Will you take a moment to pray for them now?

Most of our lives are lived in the mundane plains—the days that pass without anything remarkable happening. The plains provide a place for us to set rhythms for our lives, rhythms that don't rely on the mountaintop experiences for our faith to endure, rhythms that keep us from utter despair in the pain of our wildernesses.

Israel's rhythms centered on the tabernacle—the sacrifices, offerings, feasts, and festivals. Our rhythms center on the gathering of the believers—praying, studying the Bible, observing the Lord's Supper (Communion), participating in baptism, and keeping the Sabbath. The point of the rhythms is to keep our hearts and minds ever on the Center and Source of life—the Lord. Be assured that when we get out of rhythm, we will find ourselves drifting toward our favorite idols and off course. But also be assured that all it takes to get back into rhythm is returning to Jesus. He will wait with open arms.

How are you doing on rhythms? Have you neglected to keep them? Have you grown tired in keeping them?

If you've neglected or grown tired, I pray the Lord gives you fresh wind in your sails! I pray you know that you are never too far gone. You can always pick back up where you left off. If you're thriving in your rhythms, I pray the Lord multiplies the joy and satisfaction of intimacy with Him. If you're keeping the rhythms without much joy, I pray He ignites a fire in your bones to keep going.

No matter where you are right now, on the mountaintop, in the wilderness, or keeping the rhythms of the plain days, know that the Lord is with you. I want to close with a psalm of David. He knew the thrill of the heights, the sorrow of the depths, and the subtle danger of the plains. More than that, he knew the Lord was with him no matter what.

> O LORD, you have searched me and known me!
> You know when I sit down and when I rise up;
>> you discern my thoughts from afar.
> You search out my path and my lying down
>> and are acquainted with all my ways.
> Even before a word is on my tongue,
>> behold, O LORD, you know it altogether.
> You hem me in, behind and before,
>> and lay your hand upon me.
> Such knowledge is too wonderful for me;
>> it is high; I cannot attain it.
> Where shall I go from your Spirit?
>> Or where shall I flee from your presence?
> If I ascend to heaven, you are there!
>> If I make my bed in Sheol, you are there!
> If I take the wings of the morning
>> and dwell in the uttermost parts of the sea,
> even there your hand shall lead me,
>> and your right hand shall hold me.
> If I say, "Surely the darkness shall cover me,
>> and the light about me be night,"
> even the darkness is not dark to you;
>> the night is bright as the day,
>> for darkness is as light with you.

PSALM 139:1-12

I've provided some discussion questions here to get the conversation started. Feel free to discuss what you learned throughout the week of study, ask any questions you may have, and share what God is teaching you.

DISCUSSION QUESTIONS

Thinking back over your life, do you see God's handiwork even before you were a Christian? Tell your group about it.

What would it look like for you to make Jesus your home and allow Him to make His home in you?

Take a moment to celebrate all that you've learned in your study of the Book of Numbers. It was no easy task! What was your favorite takeaway?

Teaching sessions available for purchase or rent
at *LifeWay.com/WithUsInTheWilderness*

LEADER GUIDE

INTRODUCTION

With Us in the Wilderness: A Study of the Book of Numbers is a video- and discussion-based Bible study. The weekly personal study along with the teaching videos will promote honest conversation as you study Scripture together. Since conversation is essential to the experience, you'll find a few starter questions in both the Viewer Guides and the following Leader Guide to help get the discussion rolling.

This study may be used in a variety of large or small group settings, including churches, homes, offices, coffee shops, or other locations.

SESSION ONE

1. Welcome women to the study and distribute Bible study books.

2. Watch the Session One teaching video, encouraging women to take notes as Lauren teaches.

3. Following the video, lead participants through the discussion questions on the Session One Viewer Guide (p. 8). Remind them to complete the personal study on pages 10–45 before your group meets next time.

4. Close the session with prayer.

SESSION TWO

1. Welcome group members to Session Two of *With Us in the Wilderness.*

2. Use the following questions to review the previous week's personal study:

Which day of personal study meant the most to you? Why?

Did you learn anything in our brief recap of the books in the Pentateuch? If so, share it with the group.

If you feel comfortable, describe a time that God used a wilderness season to teach you about Himself.

What does God's pattern of dwelling with His people reveal about His character? His thoughts toward you?

Discuss what we learned this week about God's holiness—the consequences of disobedience and God's intention behind the guidelines He gives us.

What did you learn about forgiveness in this week's study? Does understanding more about God's forgiveness of you help you to forgive others or ask others to forgive you? Why or why not?

Do you find the call to be set apart (1 Cor. 7:1-7) as Christ-followers difficult or easy to live out? Explain.

3. Watch the Session Two teaching video, encouraging group members to take notes as Lauren teaches.

4. Following the video, lead participants through the discussion questions on the Session Two Viewer Guide (p. 46). Remind them to complete the personal study on pages 48–85 before your group meets next time.

5. Close: Read Numbers 6:24-26 aloud. Take a moment when you gather to speak this blessing over one another. What parts of the blessing were easy for you to receive? What parts were hard? Encourage one another to "bless" those around you.

SESSION THREE

1. Welcome group members to Session Three of *With Us in the Wilderness.*

2. Use the following questions to review the previous week's personal study:

What did you learn about the twelve days of offering that you didn't know before?

Take a moment to show off your drawing of the lampstand to the rest of the ladies in your group (p. 58). No judgment here. Way to go, artists!

Discuss some of the ways you've seen God provide for His people in Numbers thus far. Which of the provisions we've studied this week was most impactful for you? Why?

We noticed that Moses' plea for help from Hobab seems wise. How about you—when met with a challenge, do you tend to ask for too much guidance from others? Ask for too little guidance? Explain.

On Day Five, we talked a lot about discontent and complaining and God's reaction to it. Summarize the pattern that you see. How might this lesson apply to areas of restlessness in your life now?

3. Watch the Session Three teaching video, encouraging group members to take notes as Lauren teaches.

4. Following the video, lead participants through the discussion questions on the Session Three Viewer Guide (p. 86). Remind them to complete the personal study on pages 88–119 before your group meets next time.

5. Close: This week, we talked about several topics that may have hit home with the women in your group. Split into smaller groups of two or three and ask the ladies to pray for one another, specifically attending to tender spots or areas of conviction that may have been unearthed this week.

SESSION FOUR

1. Welcome group members to Session Four of *With Us in the Wilderness*.

2. Use the following questions to review the previous week's personal study:

When the spies returned from the promised land, most reported out of fear because they realized they couldn't overcome the people in Canaan in their own strength. What were they forgetting to take into account? Have you done this in your own life? Explain.

Discuss the difference between worldly grief and godly grief. How have you seen them both play out practically?

In Numbers 15 the Lord told His people to look, remember, and do—to obey God's commands out of a heart that embraces its identity as a beloved child of God. Do you find that easy to do? Or more of a challenge? Explain.

(This may be a question you want to ask group members to consider in their hearts.) If you're honest, are you more often loyal to God's kingdom or your own kingdom? If it's your kingdom, what do you think stands in the way of loyalty to God's?

3. Watch the Session Four teaching video, encouraging group members to take notes as Lauren teaches.

4. Following the video, lead participants through the discussion questions on the Session Four Viewer Guide (p. 120). Remind them to complete the personal study on pages 122–151 before your group meets next time.

5. Close: Pray for God to enable each woman in your group to walk in obedient submission to His will and ways, even when it may seem difficult or confusing. Ask God to keep you from falling when you're close to the "promised land" He wants to give you.

SESSION FIVE

1. Welcome group members to Session Five of *With Us in the Wilderness*.

2. Use the following questions to review the previous week's personal study:

When you think of the quote, "The man goes into the ground, but the message goes on," how does it make you want to live? Tell your group about the person that came to mind when you considered whom God has used in your life. (It may be the person you thanked God for on p. 130.)

Discuss the story of the fiery serpent judgment in Numbers 21. What stuck out to you?

As we read in the story of the prophet Balaam, God can use unlikely resources to move His plans forward. Tell your group about a circumstance in your life in which you need God's unlikely intervention.

Does it surprise you to hear that Balaam's prophecy in Numbers 24 foreshadowed to Jesus? What does that tell you about God's character?

Do you struggle to view sin the way God does? Do you agree with the quote, "God isn't trying to ruin your fun; He is saving your life"?

3. Watch the Session Five teaching video, encouraging group members to take notes as Lauren teaches.

4. Following the video, lead participants through the discussion questions on the Session Five Viewer Guide (p. 152). Remind them to complete the personal study on pages 154–185 before your group meets next time.

5. Close: Enlist one of the participants to close the session by praying for group members to have courage and humility to agree with God about the sin in our lives and bring it before Him, thanking Him for the forgiveness and abundant life Christ purchased for us on the cross.

SESSION SIX

1. Welcome group members to Session Six of *With Us in the Wilderness.*

2. Use the following questions to review the previous week's personal study:

How does God's faithfulness to the daughters of Zelophehad encourage you?

Have you ever been in a situation where you had to be someone's "Joshua"? Discuss the circumstance with your small group—the blessings and challenges of that season.

Which of the feasts that we studied this week was most intriguing to you? Why?

What does it practically look like for you to "put on the whole armor of God" (Eph. 6:11)? Do you practice it often? Or forget? Explain.

In Numbers 32 we read an interesting request from the people of Reuben and Gad. It led us to a discussion of motive. Take some time in your group to talk about how you've struggled with motives in your heart and judging others' motives. How can you walk free from those things?

3. Watch the Session Six teaching video, encouraging group members to take notes as Lauren teaches.

4. Following the video, lead participants through the discussion questions on the Session Six Viewer Guide (p. 186). Remind them to complete the personal study on pages 188–215 before your group meets next time.

5. Close: Pray for the women in your group to persevere in the study of Numbers, even when the lessons may seem tough. Ask God to encourage each of their hearts this week as you round out the last week of personal study.

SESSION SEVEN

1. Welcome group members to Session Seven of *With Us in the Wilderness.*

2. Use the following questions to review the previous week's personal study:

Take a few minutes to talk through your timelines with one another. (The timeline is on pp. 192–193.) Share significant moments when God provided and was present with you.

Have you struggled with the "boundaries" God has placed in your life? (Are you struggling now?) Discuss these situations with your small group and how God might be working in your heart to draw you closer to Him.

What comes to mind when you think of the unfettered fellowship we'll have with God in the new heavens and earth? How might the hope of eternity inform the things you're walking through today?

3. Watch the Session Seven teaching video, encouraging group members to take notes as Lauren teaches.

4. Following the video, lead participants through the Group Discussion section of the Session Seven Viewer Guide (p. 216).

5. Close: Wrap up the study by encouraging participants to share key truths they're taking away from the study. Be sure to discuss how they will apply what they've learned. Share your gratitude for their participation, and offer a prayer of blessing over your group as you close.

ENDNOTES

SESSION TWO

1. I was greatly helped by the introductions to each book in the *ESV Study Bible*.

2. I highly recommend Jen Wilkin's Bible studies for an in-depth look at Genesis: *God of Creation: A Study of Genesis 1–11* and *God of Covenant: A Study of Genesis 12–50*.

3. Douglas K. Stuart, *The New American Commentary: Exodus, Vol. 2* (Nashville: B&H Publishing Group, 2006), 113–114.

4. Strong's H4057, *Bible Hub*, accessed April 6, 2020, https://biblehub.com/hebrew/4057.htm.

5. BibleProject, "Overview: Leviticus," *BibleProject*, uploaded January 29, 2016, YouTube video, 8:16, accessed April 6, 2020, https://www.youtube.com/watch?v=IJ-FekWUZzE.

6. "Numbers: Note on 3:1–4:49," *ESV Study Bible*, (Wheaton, IL: Crossway, 2008).

7. Gordon J. Wenham, *Tyndale Old Testament Commentaries: Numbers, Vol. 4* , ed. D. J. Wiseman, (Downers Grove, IL: InterVarsity Press, 1981), 87, accessed via MyWSB.com.

8. "Numbers: Note on 5:5-10," *ESV Study Bible*.

9. Kenneth E. Bailey, *Jesus Through Middle Eastern Eyes: Cultural Studies in the Gospels* (Downers Grove, IL: InterVarsity Press, 2008).

10. John Piper and Wayne Grudem, *Recovering Biblical Manhood and Womanhood: A Response to Evangelical Feminism* (Wheaton, IL: Crossway Books, 1991, 2006), 126.

11. "Numbers: Note on 6:7," *ESV Study Bible*.

12. Wenham, *Numbers: Tyndale Old Testament Commentaries*, 101–102.

SESSION THREE

1. *Merriam-Webster*, s.v. "consecrate," accessed April 8, 2020, https://www.merriam-webster.com/dictionary/consecrate.

2. Strong's G4637, *Blue Letter Bible*, accessed April 8, 2020, https://www.blueletterbible.org/lang/Lexicon/Lexicon.cfm?strongs=G4637&t=KJV.

3. Strong's H1696, *Blue Letter Bible*, accessed April 8, 2020, blueletterbible.org/lang/lexicon/lexicon.cfm?Strongs=H1696&t=NLT.

4. John D. Currid, "The Lampstand," *TABLETALK*, December 2017, accessed April 8, 2020, https://tabletalkmagazine.com/article/2017/12/the-lampstand/.

5. Wenham, *Tyndale Old Testament Commentaries: Numbers*, 106.

6. John D Currid, *A Study Commentary on Numbers* (England: EP Books, 2009), 131.

7. Wenham, 113.

8. *Eerdmans Dictionary of the Bible*, ed. David Noel Freedman (Grand Rapids, MI: Wm. B. Eerdmans Publishing Co., 2000), 102.

9. Strong's H628, *Blue Letter Bible*, acessed October 6, 2020, https://www.blueletterbible.org/lang/lexicon/lexicon.cfm?t=kjv&strongs=h628.

10. Currid, *A Study Commentary on Numbers*, 156–157.

11. Ibid, 163.

SESSION FOUR

1. "Numbers: Note on 13:1–19:22," *ESV Study Bible*.

2. "II Report: Numbers 13:25-28," *NIV Standard Lesson Commentary* (Colorado Springs: Standard Publishing, 2019).

3. "Numbers: Note on 15:1-16," *ESV Study Bible*.

4. Strong's H7311, *Blue Letter Bible*, accessed April 14, 2020, https://www.blueletterbible.org/lang/lexicon/lexicon.cfm?t=kjv&strongs=h7311.

5. Wenham, 148.

6. "Smoker Identity and Its Potential Role in Young Adults' Smoking Behavior: A Meta-Ethnography," *Health Psychology: American Psychological Association*, eds. Anne E. Kazak, Ildiko Tombor, Lion Shahab, Aleksandra Herbec, Joanne Neale, Susan Michie, and Robert West, January 26, 2015,

accessed April 14, 2020, doi: 10.1037/hea0000191.

7. "Luke 8:44: NASB Lexicon," *Bible Hub*, accessed April 16, 2020, https://biblehub.com/lexicon/luke/8-44.htm.

8. "Numbers: Note on 16:20-34," *ESV Study Bible*.

9. "Numbers: Note on 17:1-13," *ESV Study Bible*.

10. Currid, 251.

11. Ibid, 255–256.

SESSION FIVE

1. Wenham, 167–168.

2. A phrase coined by Eugene Peterson.

3. "Romans: Note on 3:25," *ESV Study Bible*.

4. "Mount Hor," *Encyclopedia of The Bible*, accessed via *BibleGateway* on October 7, 2020, https://www.biblegateway.com/resources/encyclopedia-of-the-bible/Mount-Hor.

5. Wenham, 171.

6. Rev. John Brown, *A Dictionary of the Holy Bible* (London: Thomas Tegg, 1824), 475.

7. Wenham, 173.

8. Currid, 296–297.

9. Wenham, 176.

10. Dimitri Tiomkin and Ned Washington, writers, Frankie Laine, vocalist, "Rawhide," Universal Music Publishing Group, 1958.

11. "Numbers: Note on 23:1-2," *The Holman Illustrated Bible Commentary*, eds. E. Ray Clendenen and Jeremy Royal Howard (Nashville, TN: B&H Publishing Group, 2015), 161.

12. Wenham, 206.

13. John Owen, *Of the Mortification of Sin in Believers* (Woodstock, Ontario, Canada: Devoted Publishing, 2017), 9.

SESSION SIX

1. David Guizik, "Tribes of Israel – First and Second Census (Numbers 1 and 26)," *The Enduring Word Bible Commentary*, accessed August 12, 2020, https://enduringword.com/bible-commentary/numbers-26/.

2. Strong's H5270, *Blue Letter Bible*, accessed August 12, 2020, https://www.blueletterbible.org/lang/lexicon/lexicon.cfm?t=kjv&strongs=h5270.

3. Strong's H5146, *Blue Letter Bible*, accessed August 12, 2020, https://www.blueletterbible.org/lang/lexicon/lexicon.cfm?t=kjv&strongs=h5146.

4. Blair Parke, "Yeshua: Deliverer, Savior - Why This Name of God Is So Important for Today," *Bible Study Tools*, November 21, 2019, accessed August 6, 2020, https://www.biblestudytools.com/bible-study/topical-studies/yeshua-deliverer-savior.html.

5. Rev. Robert Jamieson, D.D., Rev. A. R. Fausset, A.M., and Rev. David Brown, D.D., "Acts 2:1: Notes for Verses 1-4," Jamieson-Fausset-Brown Bible Commentary (Woodside Bible Fellowship, electronic edition), accessed via MyWSB.com.

6. "Leviticus: Notes on 16:29-34; 23:26-32," *ESV Study Bible*.

7. Currid, 384.

SESSION SEVEN

1. Timothy Keller, "Introduction," *Counterfeit Gods: The Empty Promises of Money, Sex, and Power, and the Only Hope That Matters* (New York: Penguin Books, 2009), xix–xx.